# GameMaker Essentials

Learn all the essential skills of GameMaker:
Studio and start making your own impressive
games with ease

**Nathan Auckett**

BIRMINGHAM - MUMBAI

# GameMaker Essentials

First published: March 2015

Production reference: 1230315

Published by Packt Publishing Ltd.
Livery Place
35 Livery Street
Birmingham B3 2PB, UK.

ISBN 978-1-78439-612-1

www.packtpub.com

# Credits

**Author**
Nathan Auckett

**Reviewers**
Mark Alexander
John M. Walker, PE

**Commissioning Editor**
Nadeem N. Bagban

**Acquisition Editor**
Harsha Bharwani

**Content Development Editor**
Samantha Gonsalves

**Technical Editor**
Bharat Patil

**Copy Editors**
Relin Hedly
Laxmi Subramanian

**Project Coordinator**
Sanchita Mandal

**Proofreaders**
Simran Bhogal
Lauren E. Harkins

**Indexer**
Hemangini Bari

**Production Coordinator**
Conidon Miranda

**Cover Work**
Conidon Miranda

# About the Author

**Nathan Auckett** is an advanced GameMaker user and has been using the software for over 7 years now. He started using GameMaker during its seventh version and has been using the built-in programming language ever since to create his own games. In 2012, he began creating small tutorials on various topics in GameMaker and has since then created over 50 tutorials helping people achieve a variety of different tasks in GameMaker.

# About the Reviewers

**Mark Alexander** is a self-taught programmer and writer. He started using BASIC on an old ZX81 and progressed through the years using other languages and learning the tools of the programming trade until he discovered GameMaker in 2006. At that point, he fell in love with the software and now dedicates his time to making games and writing articles on using the program and on game design in general.

Mark currently documents products for YoYo Games (who makes and sells GameMaker: Studio) and also has his own small software company, Nocturne Games, which specializes in small, family-friendly, and quirky games for all platforms.

Mark was the technical editor of *GameMaker: Studio For Dummies, For Dummies* as well as *Learning GML* from the *Game Maker* book series.

**John M. Walker, PE** is a licensed professional engineer in industrial engineering and is currently a licensed full-time teacher in computer science and information technology at Gresham High School near Portland, OR. He has been teaching full time for the last 15 years for High School and Regional Professional Higher Ed conferences.

John worked for more than 20 years as an information technology manager for high technology firms dealing with systems administration and networking architecture and engineering. His favorite designation was Director of Technology for the Portland Trail Blazers, while designing and constructing the Moda Center.

# www.PacktPub.com

## Support files, eBooks, discount offers, and more

For support files and downloads related to your book, please visit www.PacktPub.com.

Did you know that Packt offers eBook versions of every book published, with PDF and ePub files available? You can upgrade to the eBook version at www.PacktPub.com, and as a print book customer, you are entitled to a discount on the eBook copy. Get in touch with us at service@packtpub.com for more details.

At www.PacktPub.com, you can also read a collection of free technical articles, sign up for a range of free newsletters, and receive exclusive discounts and offers on Packt books and eBooks.

https://www2.packtpub.com/books/subscription/packtlib

Do you need instant solutions to your IT questions? PacktLib is Packt's online digital book library. Here, you can search, access, and read Packt's entire library of books.

## Why subscribe?

- Fully searchable across every book published by Packt
- Copy and paste, print, and bookmark content
- On-demand and accessible via a web browser

## Free access for Packt account holders

If you have an account with Packt at www.PacktPub.com, you can use this to access PacktLib today and view nine entirely free books. Simply use your login credentials for immediate access.

# Table of Contents

# Preface

Welcome to *GameMaker Essentials*. This book will teach you how to use GameMaker: Studio to create your very own games from start to finish. You will learn the very basics, such as how to use the GameMaker: Studio interface, as well as the more advanced features such as programming, monetizing your game, and finally exporting your game for publishing.

If you have ever wanted to create your own games for operating systems, such as Windows, Android, iOS, Linux, and more, then this book is the perfect place to start.

## What this book covers

*Chapter 1, Introducing GameMaker*, introduces GameMaker: Studio by telling us exactly what it is and the basic idea behind it. The chapter also looks into some of GameMaker's history as well as showing how to install it onto your computer.

*Chapter 2, Getting Started*, walks you through the GameMaker: Studio interface, teaching you what each button does and introducing you to some of the core aspects of the interface.

*Chapter 3, Resource Management*, teaches you how to manage resources. In this chapter, you will learn what each resource is and also the best practices in organizing resources.

*Chapter 4, Objects*, introduces you to one of the core resources in GameMaker, objects. You will learn about the object interface and also how they function.

*Chapter 5, The GameMaker Language*, teaches you how to program using GameMaker's very own programming language. By the end of this chapter, you will be ready to program your own game.

*Chapter 6, Sprites*, takes a detailed look at the sprite resource in GameMaker. You will learn how to create sprites, edit sprites, the good sizing techniques, and finally, how to change the way sprites act through programming.

*Chapter 7, Making a Game*, walks you through the process of making your very own game using GameMaker Language (GML). You will learn more about rooms, objects, programming, and common practices in this chapter.

*Chapter 8, Debugging*, teaches you about debugging in GameMaker. You will learn how to read an error report, how to draw information to the screen, how to enable simple toggles, and finally, how to use the GameMaker debugger.

*Chapter 9, Game Settings and Exporting*, covers the settings available for each game in GameMaker. You will also learn how to implement ads, analytics, how to export your game, and also how to publish your final game.

# What you need for this book

For this book, you will need:

- An active Internet connection
- GameMaker: Studio (free version or higher)

# Who this book is for

If you are an experienced developer or a beginner who wants to enter the rich world and experience of GameMaker: Studio, then this book is ideal for you.

# Conventions

In this book, you will find a number of text styles that distinguish between different kinds of information. Here are some examples of these styles and an explanation of their meaning.

Code words in text, database table names, folder names, filenames, file extensions, pathnames, dummy URLs, user input, and Twitter handles are shown as follows: "We can include other contexts through the use of the `include` directive."

**New terms** and **important words** are shown in bold. Words that you see on the screen, for example, in menus or dialog boxes, appear in the text like this: "To do this, right-click on any branch and choose **Create Group**."

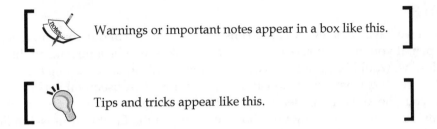

Warnings or important notes appear in a box like this.

Tips and tricks appear like this.

# Reader feedback

Feedback from our readers is always welcome. Let us know what you think about this book—what you liked or disliked. Reader feedback is important for us as it helps us develop titles that you will really get the most out of.

To send us general feedback, simply e-mail feedback@packtpub.com and mention the book's title in the subject of your message.

If there is a topic that you have expertise in and you are interested in either writing or contributing to a book, see our author guide at www.packtpub.com/authors.

# Customer support

Now that you are the proud owner of a Packt book, we have a number of things to help you to get the most from your purchase.

## Downloading the color images of this book

We also provide you with a PDF file that has color images of the screenshots/ diagrams used in this book. The color images will help you better understand the changes in the output. You can download this file from https://www.packtpub. com/sites/default/files/downloads/6121OS_ColorImages.pdf.

# Errata

Although we have taken every care to ensure the accuracy of our content, mistakes do happen. If you find a mistake in one of our books—maybe a mistake in the text or the code—we would be grateful if you could report this to us. By doing so, you can save other readers from frustration and help us improve subsequent versions of this book. If you find any errata, please report them by visiting http://www.packtpub.com/submit-errata, selecting your book, clicking on the **Errata Submission Form** link, and entering the details of your errata. Once your errata are verified, your submission will be accepted and the errata will be uploaded to our website or added to any list of existing errata under the Errata section of that title.

To view the previously submitted errata, go to https://www.packtpub.com/books/content/support and enter the name of the book in the search field. The required information will appear under the **Errata** section.

# Piracy

Piracy of copyrighted material on the Internet is an ongoing problem across all media. At Packt, we take the protection of our copyright and licenses very seriously. If you come across any illegal copies of our works in any form on the Internet, please provide us with the location address or website name immediately so that we can pursue a remedy.

Please contact us at copyright@packtpub.com with a link to the suspected pirated material.

We appreciate your help in protecting our authors and our ability to bring you valuable content.

# Questions

If you have a problem with any aspect of this book, you can contact us at questions@packtpub.com, and we will do our best to address the problem.

# 1
# Introducing GameMaker

In this chapter, you will learn what GameMaker is all about, who made it, what it is used for, and more. You will then also be learning how to install GameMaker on your computer that is ready for use.

In this chapter, we will cover the following topics:

- Understanding GameMaker
- Installing GameMaker: Studio
- What is this book about?

## Understanding GameMaker

Before getting started with GameMaker, it is best to know exactly what it is and what it's designed to do.

GameMaker is a 2D game creation software by YoYo Games. It was designed to allow anyone to easily develop games without having to learn complex programming languages such as C++ through the use of its drag and drop functionality.

The drag and drop functionality allows the user to create games by visually organizing icons on screen, which represent actions and statements that will occur during the game.

GameMaker also has a built-in programming language called **GameMaker Language**, or **GML** for short. GML allows users to type out code to be run during their game. All drag and drop actions are actually made up of this GML code.

GameMaker is primarily designed for 2D games, and most of its features and functions are designed for 2D game creation. However, GameMaker does have the ability to create 3D games and has a number of functions dedicated to this.

# GameMaker: Studio

There are a number of different versions of GameMaker available, most of which are unsupported because they are outdated; however, support can still be found in the GameMaker Community Forums. GameMaker: Studio is the first version of GameMaker after GameMaker HTML5 to allow users to create games and export them for use on multiple devices and operating systems including PC, Mac, Linux, and Android, on both mobile and desktop versions.

GameMaker: Studio is designed to allow one code base (GML) to run on any device with minimal changes to the base code. Users are able to export their games to run on any supported device or system such as HTML5 without changing any code to make things work.

GameMaker: Studio was also the first version available for download and use through the Steam marketplace. YoYo Games took advantage of the Steam workshop and allowed Steam-based users to post and share their creations through the service.

GameMaker: Studio is sold in a number of different versions, which include several enhanced features and capabilities as the price gets higher.

The standard version is free to download and use. However, it lacks some advanced features included in higher versions and only allows for exporting to the Windows desktop.

The professional version is the second cheapest from the standard version. It includes all features, but only has the Windows desktop and Windows app exports. Other exports can be purchased at an extra cost ranging from $99.99 to $300.

The master version is the most expensive of all the options. It comes with every feature and every export, including all future export modules in version 1.*x*. If you already own exports in the professional version, you can get the prices of those exports taken off the price of the master version.

# Installing GameMaker: Studio

Installing GameMaker is performed much like any other program. In this case, we will be installing GameMaker: Studio as this is the most up-to-date version at this point.

You can find the download at the YoYo Games website, `https://www.yoyogames.com/`.

From the site, you can pick the free version or purchase one of the others. All the installations are basically the same.

Once the installer is downloaded, we are ready to install GameMaker: Studio. This is just like installing any other program. Just run the file, and then follow the on-screen instructions to accept the license agreement, choose an install location, and install the software.

On the first run, you may see a progress bar appear at the top left of your screen. This is just GameMaker running its first time setup. It will also do this during the update process as YoYo Games releases new features.

Once it is done, you should see a welcome screen and will be prompted to enter your registration code. The key should be e-mailed to you when you make an account during the purchase/download process. Enter this key and your copy of GameMaker: Studio should be registered. You may be prompted to restart GameMaker at this time. Close GameMaker and re-open it and you should see the welcome screen and be able to choose from a number of options on it:

# What is this book about?

We now have GameMaker: Studio installed and are ready to get started with it.

In this book, we will be covering the essential things to know about GameMaker: Studio. This includes everything from drag and drop actions to programming in GameMaker using GameMaker Language (GML). You will learn about how things in GameMaker are structured, and how to organize resources to keep things as clean as possible. By the end of the book, we would have made a simple functioning game and will be ready to get going with game development using GameMaker: Studio.

# Summary

In this chapter, we looked into what GameMaker actually is and learned that there are different versions available. We also looked at the different types of GameMaker: Studio available for download and purchase. We then learned how to install GameMaker: Studio, which is the final step in getting ready to learn the essential skills and starting to make our very own games.

In the next chapter, we will look into creating a new project and the main interfaces of GameMaker: Studio.

# 2
# Getting Started

In this chapter, we will be looking into the main interface of GameMaker: Studio and exploring the functions and features available within the program.

In this chapter, we will cover the following topics:

- Licensing
- The welcome window
- The main toolbar
- The drop-down menus
- The resource tree

## Licensing

With GameMaker: Studio installed, it is important to know exactly what your license gives you in terms of access.

Firstly, your license key grants you an access to GameMaker. It also provides proof of purchase if you have one of the paid versions.

Your key also provides you with access to any export modules you have purchased. When purchasing a module, your key will be updated and you will need to enter the updated key into GameMaker for your new features to take effect.

To do this, GameMaker has an **Update License** option under the **Help** drop-down button as shown in the screenshot given here:

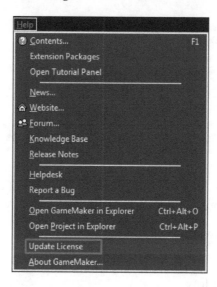

Clicking on this will show a dialog where you may enter your new license key. You will then be prompted to restart GameMaker: Studio to finish the process. Once that is done, you should have access to your purchased features and modules.

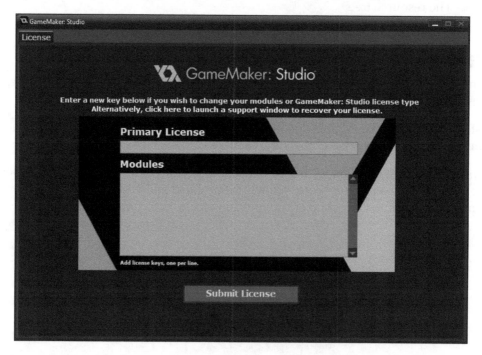

If you ever need to re-register GameMaker for any reason and need your license key/keys, you can have them e-mailed to you via the YoYo Games website on the support page. Simply enter your e-mail address to have an automated e-mail sent to you containing your license keys and related information. It is also advised to keep a backup of your email and license key in a safe place.

# The welcome window

The welcome window is the first window you see every time you open GameMaker: Studio. Here you can see tips on GameMaker: Studio's use, and also your most recently opened projects. To load one of these projects, simply click on it in the list.

The welcome window also has a few other features built into it. At the top of the window, there are nine tabs all labeled based on the functions they provide. The description of each tab is as follows:

- **Open**: This allows you to browse and open a GameMaker file.
- **New**: This allows you to start a new project by entering a name and saving at a desired location.

- **Import**: This allows you to import a project from a previous version of GameMaker or backup file. You may also load GameMaker Zip (GMZ) files here. These files are full project packages often used to easily send or back up a project.

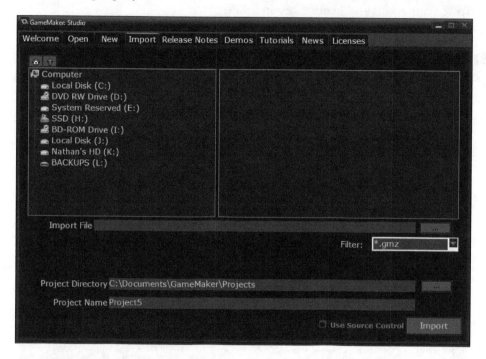

- **Release Notes**: This shows the release notes for the currently used version of GameMaker.
- **Demos**: This has a selection of downloadable demo projects with completely open source files, allowing for an easy jump start to your own project.
- **Tutorials**: This has a selection of downloadable tutorial projects teaching various skills and techniques.
- **News**: This shows the most recent news on the YoYo Games website.
- **Licenses**: This shows licensing information from the software included and used within GameMaker.

These tabs provide fast access to all of GameMaker's information and file management functions.

# The main toolbar

The main toolbar is where you can find the creation buttons for every essential resource as well as saving and exporting settings. Everything on the toolbar can also be accessed from the drop-down menus; however, the toolbar creates a fast and easy way of accessing these functions in as little time as possible. Hovering your mouse over any of the icons on the main toolbar will show basic information stating what the button does.

In the first section of the toolbar, you have your project functions, including the new project, the load project, and the save project. We will be covering the sections based on the separation lines shown in between the icons.

The second section only has one button. This button exports your project to the designated target module. To change the target module, you can use the "Target" drop-down menu found to the right of all the icons on the main toolbar.

The third section holds your testing functions. This includes playing a test build in both normal and debug mode, stopping the web server, and clearing the cache. Debug mode allows you to get detailed information on the game as it runs, for example, seeing where resources are being used and tracking variables. The web server is GameMaker's micro web server. This runs when testing on the HTML5 module or when testing on a mobile device over Wi-Fi. The cache is where GameMaker stores resource information, making compiling faster after the first time around. If you ever see strange graphical issues, it is advised to clear the cache and re-compile as this may be obsolete data that is being loaded.

The fourth section allows you to access the global game settings and also manage extensions. The GameMaker Global Game Settings are the main settings for any GameMaker made game. They hold all essential data for every export type. Extensions are user-made extensions that can add extra functionality to GameMaker and your games, in turn. These are used for advertising APIs for mobile or HTML5-based games.

# The drop-down menus

The drop-down menus provide access to almost everything on the main menu, as well as a few extra functions.

File   Edit   Window   Resources   Scripts   Run   Marketplace Beta   Help

These functions include the following:

- The **File** menu gives you access to functions regarding the main settings of GameMaker, and also loading and exporting options.
- The **Edit** toolbar gives you access to functions regarding the editing and management of resources in GameMaker games.
- The **Window** drop-down menu gives access to functions to control the active resource windows in GameMaker.
- The **Resources** menu holds all the functions of the main toolbar, excluding configuration and export modules. It also has an option of defining macros. Macros are constant variables in GameMaker. You define them in the table that is shown after choosing **Define Macros** in this drop-down menu and you can then use them throughout your game.

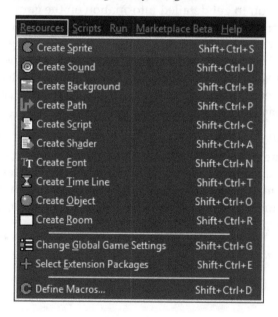

- The **Scripts** menu gives access to functions regarding scripts and also built-in variables in GameMaker. In this menu, you are able to search through scripts for keywords or entire functions. You can also initialize a resource name check to ensure there are no duplicate names.

- The **Run** menu provides access to all the run functions available on the main toolbar.

- The **Marketplace** menu provides access to options related to the GameMaker marketplace where GameMaker users can upload, sell, download, and purchase assets created in GameMaker.

- The **Help** drop-down menu provides access to the GameMaker help file, information on your license key, and also links to the GameMaker website, including **News** and **Forum**. You may also open the folder GameMaker is installed in and open the folder the current project is saved in for quick and easy access.

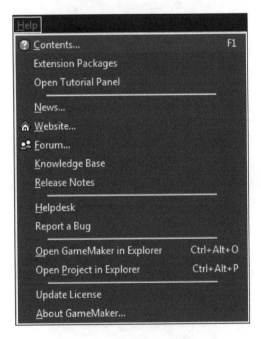

# The resource tree

The resource tree is one of the main aspects of the GameMaker user interface. Here, you can find every resource of your game ordered by its type and also custom-made branches.

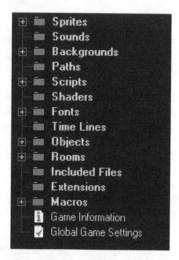

To start with, you will have empty branches labeled with every resource type available. Resources will be automatically put into their designated base branches, but you can create new sub-branches to further organize them.

To do this, right-click on any branch and choose **Create Group**. You will then be prompted to give a name. Once the branch is created, simply drag a resource onto it to add it in the new group.

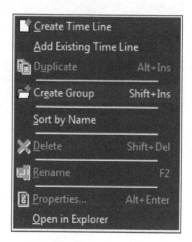

The resource tree also stores and gives access to any included files that may be necessary for your game such as DLL files or images, as well as extension functions. Extensions are created directly within the resource tree by right-clicking on the extensions branch.

To access a resource from the tree, simply double-click on the resource name.

# Summary

In this chapter, we learned about the main interface of GameMaker, and we are now ready to get started with using GameMaker and its features.

We are now able to access every function regarding resources and GameMaker functionality, as well as how resources are sorted within the GameMaker user interface.

In the next chapter, we will begin looking at resource management and what resources are actually there in GameMaker.

# 3

# Resource Management

In this chapter, we will be looking at GameMaker's resources and ways to organize and manage them while creating a game. It is extremely important to keep projects organized while creating them. This is because the more resources you add to a project, the more confusing it will become to remember what each one is for and where they are positioned in the resource tree.

The following is the screenshot of an unorganized project:

The following is the screenshot of an organized project:

As you can see, the organized project is well sorted and clearly labeled, whereas the unorganized project has resources spread out and is confusing to look at.

In this chapter, we will look at techniques for organizing resources so that our projects are always as easy as possible to keep track of.

# Resources in GameMaker

GameMaker has a number of resources that are made available to its users. These resources or assets are what we use to create games within GameMaker. A resource in GameMaker is essentially anything that is used within the game. This includes sprites, backgrounds, objects, scripts, fonts, sounds, rooms, and more.

We will go through the available resources and learn a bit more about each of them so that we can take full advantage of each one.

# Sprites

Sprites can be seen as an image loaded into GameMaker to allow for visual representations in a game. For example, a player animation would most commonly be loaded as a sprite, or multiple sprites.

A sprite is in most cases either a single image or an animation sequence consisting of multiple images. This could be anything from a wall to a character running or jumping.

Sprites are commonly referenced on the Internet, especially on game development sites. Sprites are not specific to GameMaker alone and can be heard of or referenced in many other places.

A sprite can be any image. It does not have to be a certain size or format; it simply needs to be imported or created as a sprite resource in GameMaker for it to be considered a sprite. A sprite can even be used as a background if need be. This is most commonly seen when the background has some sort of looping animation.

Here is an example of a sprite in GameMaker:

As you can see in the preceding screenshot, the sprite is a series of separate images forming an animation. The animation starts at the top-left image and continues through to the bottom-right image before starting again.

A sprite does not need any animation; here is a single image sprite:

The preceding sprite is a simple rock. It is only one static image but is still considered to be a sprite.

# Sounds

Sounds are fairly self-explanatory. A sound resource in GameMaker can be any kind of sound, including sound effects and background music. Any sound in GameMaker is normally played through the use of the sound resource.

The following is the screenshot of a sound resource in GameMaker:

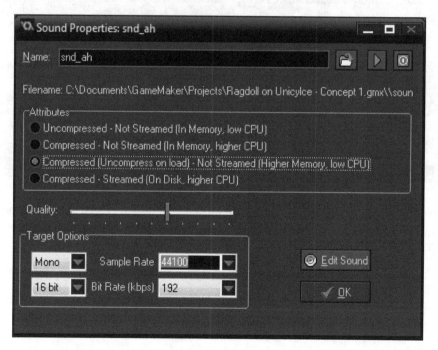

The preceding screenshot shows a simple sound effect used as a pain sound. In the sound properties window, you can change a number of options for a sound.

Under attributes, you can change the sound's compression options; each option has a different end effect. Some cause the CPU to be of higher use while others cause a larger file size in the final game.

You can also adjust the quality and playback settings in this window.

Common formats used in GameMaker include OGG, MP3, and WAV.

OGG and MP3 files are better for music as they are highly compressed but still retain a good amount of sound quality. The compression allows for a smaller file size in the final game.

WAV files are normally better for sound effects. They are uncompressed sound files, meaning no quality is lost at all. Due to most sound effects being short in length, the extra file size doesn't normally have a large impact on the file size itself.

# Backgrounds

Backgrounds are also fairly self-explanatory. However, there are a few extra tasks backgrounds are used for.

The first task is tiles. Tiles are normally used to organize a set of ground or scenery graphics into a single image. GameMaker uses backgrounds to load tiles and split them into grid style segments. These can then be placed in your game levels using the room editor.

The second task backgrounds can be used for is textures. Although GameMaker is focused on 2D game creation, it does have the ability to create 3D games as well. Backgrounds are used as textures in 3D games. For best results when doing this, the backgrounds and dimensions should be set at a power of two, for example, 8, 16, 32, 64, and so on.

# Paths

In GameMaker, paths are used to define a path that an object may follow during the game. This comes in handy, for example, with tower defense-style games when you need to make the enemies follow a path. To make path creation easier, you can view a room directly in the path editor and use that to make the path bypass certain obstacles that may be present.

Creating a path is simple due to its creation being visually based. To create a new path, click on the button on the main toolbar that looks like a green line with an arrow at the end .

This will bring up the path properties window, where you can create your path. From this point, creating a path is as simple as clicking on places in the grid to add a new point to the path.

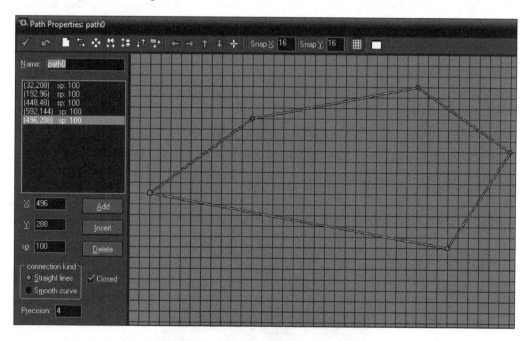

As you can see in the preceding image, each point has a yellow line going between them better displaying the path an object would follow.

Every time you create a new point, a new item is added to the list in the top left of the preceding graph. This list shows the exact $x$ and $y$ positions of the point added as well as the speed multiplier. The speed multiplier allows you to make an object speed up or slow down along a path.

At the bottom left of the graph, you can see extra options for your path. You can manually type positions and click on the **Add** button to add a new section to the path. You can also uncheck the **Closed** box to make the path an open shape instead of automatically looping back to the first point.

If you want a smooth path, you can change the connection kind to **Smooth curve** instead of the default, **Straight lines**. This will make the curve smooth along the corners.

Here is an example of a smooth path:

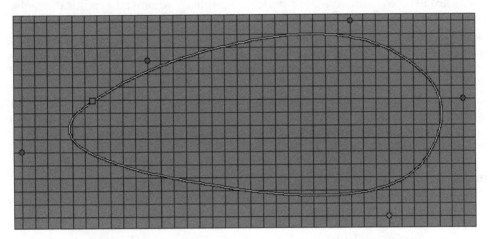

As you can see, the points are in the same position but the actual path is smooth and curved instead of being jagged along each point.

If you want to display a certain room on the path properties window so that you can create a path through certain objects, click on the blank window icon at the end of

the main toolbar and then select the room you wish to display ▢.

# Scripts

Scripts are one of the most useful things when programming in GameMaker. A script is basically a code block that can be accessed by any object at any time during the game.

They become extremely useful when multiple objects need to execute the same code. Instead of copying the code into each object, you can create a script with the code in it and simply type the script name into the object instead of the entire code. Then, if there is an error within that script, you only need to change one piece of code instead of many throughout each object.

Scripts can also be used to create your own functions. Using arguments, you can make a script that allows for input when it is run by an object. You can also return a value back to the object from a script. You can take advantage of this when performing complicated math functions that require a value to be saved for the future. You can type the math code into a script and then save it to a variable when it is run by returning the value.

# Shaders

Shaders are used in GameMaker to perform simple or advanced graphical effects. This includes everything from a real-time Gaussian blur to 2D and 3D lighting. Shaders are extremely powerful and work by directly editing things that are being drawn by the GPU. When no shader is applied, GameMaker will still draw sprites and backgrounds using a default shader that has no effect on the graphics.

A GPU, stands for graphics processing unit, is more often called a graphics card. It is a device that allows a computer to draw a display onto a computer monitor. The more graphics that need to be drawn to the screen at once, the faster and better a GPU needs to be to handle it all.

GameMaker uses open GLSL ES by default; however, it also accepts regular GLSL, HLSL, and PSSL as its shader language and the limitations really depend on the user's knowledge of the selected language.

GLSL stands for OpenGL Shading Language. GLSL is a high-level shading language based on the syntax of C programming and allows developers to have more direct control of the graphics pipeline, using a more commonly known language structure.

The graphics pipeline is the queue of graphics that are to be drawn by the GPU at any one time.

# Fonts

In GameMaker, you can use events to draw directly to the screen while your game runs. Part of this includes drawing text, and where there is text, there is a font. A font in GameMaker is simply a predefined character set that can be used while drawing text in your game. This can be used for drawing dialog or instructions.

# Timelines

A timeline is essentially a timer with different events set throughout, which is at times defined by the user. For example, you may create an object when 30 steps have passed, and then make that object move after another 30 steps.

Timelines are extremely useful for precise event timing through GameMaker games, especially when you need things to happen multiple times for multiple instances.

# Objects

The second most important resource in any GameMaker game, with the first most important being a room, is an object. Simply speaking, without objects, you don't have a game in GameMaker.

An object works by use of predefined events that are built into GameMaker. Within events are user-defined actions that control what the object does. Through the use of actions, a user can make an object move, jump, fall, and more.

An object allows users to easily create individual pieces for their game. This can be anything from the main character that is controlled by the player, to an enemy that chases the player if they get too close.

Objects hold all the code and allow us to easily organize and visualize what is going to happen when the game runs. This makes programming in GameMaker much easier than in some other engines.

Objects are abstract entities that act as a blueprint from which instances are created. This means you can have one object, but multiple instances of that object in your room, for example, a coin or an enemy.

The following screenshot is an example of an object in GameMaker:

# Rooms

Rooms are the number one most important part of a GameMaker game. The reason for this is because without a room, you can't even run your game.

A room can be seen as the window of a GameMaker game. All GameMaker games happen within at least one, if not more. Rooms are where we place our objects and run our code. When designing a level in GameMaker, you are using the room editor. The room editor shows up when you create a new room, or select a room for editing. Within the editor, you can change the way the game is viewed by the player and design your levels.

You may only have one room active at a time; you cannot have the game run in multiple rooms at once.

# Extensions

GameMaker has the ability to load external functions and use them within the game. This is done by use of an extension. Extensions are made by GameMaker users and can include anything from a JavaScript file to a DLL. This allows for new and advanced functions to be made and imported into GameMaker.

Most extensions work using an external library of functions. This external library, for example, a DLL file, is added into a project through the use of the extension resource. From there, functions are set up in GameMaker, allowing the user to access the new functions within the external library.

This allows for an endless possibility of functions within GameMaker as they can be used to do things such as accessing the camera on a mobile device to controlling media on a personal computer.

Extensions have been made to allow the use of many software development kits from a number of companies, as well as access social sites such as GameJolt for achievements and high scores.

# Macros

In other programming languages, you may have heard of or even used a data type called a **constant**. Macros are GameMaker's version of a constant data type.

A macro, or constant, is a data type that never changes and often stores a value. These values have a global scope, which means they can be accessed by any instance within a game. They are commonly used to easily define things such as weapon types using numbers instead of strings.

A handgun could be considered gun type 0. A machine gun could be gun type 1. Instead of checking a string to see what gun type is currently being held by the character in a game, you can check what gun they are holding based on the name of the macro variable.

Here is an example in GML code:

```
if gun_type=HANDGUN{
    //do something
}
if gun_type=MACHINEGUN{
    //do something
}
```

HANDGUN and MACHINEGUN are macro variables. HANDGUN is equal to 0 and MACHINEGUN is equal to 1. Without the macros, that code would look like the following:

```
if gun_type=0{
    //do something
}
if gun_type=1
    //do something
```

As you can see by comparing the preceding two images, macros allow for the code to be easily read by the programmer, making it more organized and easier to keep track of.

Macro variables cannot be changed, which means once the value is set, you may not change the value of the variable later on in the game.

# Resource naming conventions

While working with GameMaker, you will begin to see how important it is to keep things as organized as possible. Part of this is keeping resource names short and concise. If your resource names are long and complicated, it can lead to ugly and confusing code later on.

Due to GameMaker having specific resources, it becomes easy to keep resource names clean. The easiest and most commonly used way to keep names consistent and specific to each resource type is to pick a code word or letter to put in front of the actual resource name.

When looking at other GameMaker projects, you will see a few different implementations of this. We are going to take a look at the three-letter code word technique. This is where you pick a three-letter code word to put in front of your resource name. The code word should be specific to each resource type. There is no need to stick to three letters. You can use one, two, or more letters if you want to.

Here are some commonly used three-letter code words that are used:

- `spr` for Sprite
- `snd` for Sound
- `bck` for Background
- `pth` for Path
- `scr` for Script
- `shd` for Shader
- `fnt` for Font
- `tml` for Time Line
- `obj` for Object
- `rm` for Room

These are the most common abbreviations for three-letter code words. You might have noticed that the code word for a room is only two letters. You can use three letters if you want, but there is no need to do so for such a simple word.

Okay, so now that we have seen the code words, how are these structured into resource names? You put the code words in front of your resource name, separated by an underscore ("_"). So for an object, it might be called `obj_player`, where `obj` is the code word. This is the same for every other resource type.

The reason naming things this way is so useful is because it allows you to name resources of different types with the same title. For example, you might have an object called `player` and also a sprite called `player`. This would actually cause an error in GameMaker as you are not allowed to have two resources with the same name. The code words make the names different, and allow for you to easily see what kind of resource is being mentioned when reading over the code.

# Organizing resources

There are a few different ways to keep resources organized in GameMaker.

The first, as in the previous topic, is using naming conventions. These allow you to easily distinguish between different kinds of resources and also link them by name.

We are going to take a look at a few more techniques to organize things and make our games easier to navigate.

## Groups

The first technique is using groups in the resource tree. If you right-click on a resource or a resource folder in the resource tree, you will find a **Create Group** option. Clicking on this will bring up a small dialog asking you to enter a name for the group. Simply enter a name and click on **OK.** A new folder should then show up in the tree and you can click and drag resources into that folder.

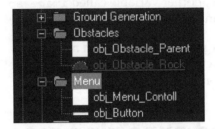

When doing this, group your objects by similarities. If you have objects used only in one room of your game, think about naming the group based on that room. For example, you might put menu objects in a group called **Menu**. You can also group objects based on what they are, for example, putting spikes and rocks into a group called **Obstacles**, trees and shrubs into a group called Scenery, or different enemies into a group called Enemies. Try to keep group names simple, and avoid going overboard with groups as this can just cause more clutter. Groups do not affect the game in any way, they are only a visual tool for keeping the resource tree organized.

## Sprite animations

When it comes to sprites, there is another way of keeping things organized. It is much the same as using groups; however, instead you are using an actual resource to group things together.

Let's say we have a set of walls. All are static (nonanimated) images but have different looks to them. We could have all these different walls saved as separate sprites, or we could put them all into one sprite as an animation. What this does is allow us to have all the nonanimated wall images in one resource as if it were a group.

When attaching this to an object, by default, it would play through every wall image as an animation and would look a bit weird in the game. To avoid this, we need to stop the animation, and then pick which wall image we actually want to use. To achieve this, we can use GML code or a drag and drop action to set the animation speed to 0 and stop the animation. However, we still have the issue of actually picking which image we want to show. For this, GameMaker has a variable unique to each object called image_index. Each frame of a sprite is referenced as a number from 0 upwards, 0 being the first frame of every sprite resource. To choose which image we want to show, we just have to set the image index, which can be done in GML or using a drag and drop action.

The image index of an object is separate to the animation speed. To actually stop the animation, we need to set another variable called image_speed to 0. This stops the animation from progressing through frames.

While this technique of organization may seem more complicated, it can actually make code and game structure easier if used correctly. Whether this technique should be used depends on the game being made.

# Importing and exporting resources

When it comes to importing resources to GameMaker, it can be done in two ways. The first way is by importing a graphic or sound into GameMaker to be used later in a game. The second is by importing an actual GameMaker resource.

## Importing graphics and sounds

Loading graphics to be used as a resource in your game can be done in three different ways. You can either create a new sprite and click on the **load sprite** button on the interface that appears, create a new background and click on **load background** on the interface that appears, or you can drag and drop your graphic from Windows Explorer onto the GameMaker interface and pick which resource type you want it to be from the dialog that appears.

The same can be done with sound. You can either create a new sound resource and load your sound from the interface that appears, or you can drag the sound file from Windows Explorer onto the GameMaker interface.

# Importing GameMaker resources

When creating any kind of resource in GameMaker, the source is saved in a structure of folders under the location of your saved project file. These folders include every resource type and organize them. Each resource saves certain information in the form of a GMX file, which is an editable XML-style document. Resources such as sprites will also have the graphic saved with them.

GameMaker allows you to import these saved GMX files into other projects as you wish. This means if you have made a fully functioning player in one project and need it for another, you don't have to remake it. Instead, you can just import the resource from the other project.

To do this, simply right-click on the resource type you want to import in the resource tree. On the drop-down menu that comes up, choose the **Add Existing [Resource type]** option. You can then browse through your folders using Windows Explorer and find the resource you want to import from a different project. This can be done for any resource type.

# Exporting resources

Due to the way GameMaker saves its project files, all resources are already exported as a GMX file and stored within the project folder. To view these files, open up your default file browser and go to the directory that holds your saved project. Your project will be saved within a structure of folders, each one being organized based on the resource types in your project, such as objects and sprites.

Here is an example of how this looks in Windows Explorer:

GameMaker also has the option to export the entire project as a GMZ file, which is a compressed version of the GMX file that saves space and makes it easier to share projects with other people, for example, a team member.

To do this, click on the file drop-down list at the top left of the GameMaker interface and choose the **Export Project** option. This will display Windows Explorer, allowing you to choose where to export the project.

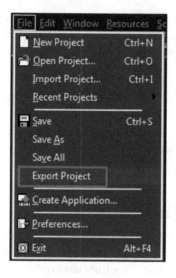

# Exporting scripts

While scripts are saved the same way as all other resources in GameMaker, we also have the extra option to export them as GML files for use in other projects.

To export a script to a GML file, right-click on the script in the resource tree and choose the **Export Selected Script** option in the drop-down list. This will display a new window wherein you can choose where to save your exported script.

You can also export entire groups of scripts by right-clicking on a group of scripts and then choosing the **-Export Group of Scripts-** option from the drop-down list.

This will generate a text file with the .gml extension, which can be edited in any text editor, such as Notepad.

# Summary

In this chapter, we learned about GameMaker's resources and what they are all used for within GameMaker. We also learned how to manage resources within our GameMaker projects through the use of naming conventions and groups. Finally, we learned how to import and export GameMaker resources and how GameMaker projects are structured when they are saved.

We can now get started with the actual game making process within GameMaker.

# 4
# Objects

In this chapter, we will take a look at the object resource in GameMaker. We will look at how they are structured, how they work, and what can be done with them. We will then use the drag and drop functions to create a simple game and broaden our understanding of how objects work.

## Events

When it comes to objects, it is extremely important to know what an event is. This is due to pretty much everything in a GameMaker game happening within some sort of event.

In general, an event is often referred to as a thing that happens, or takes place; often times, the event is of some sort of importance. For example, you may attend an athletics event. In GameMaker, it is much the same. GameMaker has a number of predefined events that allow us to easily make things happen when certain other events take place or when something happens in the game, for example, a mouse button being pressed.

As an example, we will look at the first event of any object, the create event. The create event is triggered when an instance is created within a room. It is always the first event to be executed. The create event is commonly used to initialize variables for later use in an instance, for example, a score variable.

How is an event triggered? In most cases, it is automatically triggered by GameMaker itself. When an instance is first created, the create event of that instance is automatically run. However, it is possible to manually trigger an event using GameMaker Language code.

This is a piece of code manually triggering a create event:

```
event_perform(ev_create,0);
```

# The step event

One of the most useful events after the create event is the step event. The step event runs within an object at every step of the game. You can look at a step like a frame in the game. In every frame of the game, one step is run within every object that is active during that frame. The step event is where you will have the game logic that needs to be checked constantly, for example, key presses, collisions, or tracking the amount of lives the player has left.

# Room speed

A game's targeted refresh rate in GameMaker is controlled by the room speed. This is how many steps are meant to run every second. This is not guaranteed, as on a low-end device, the CPU may simply not be able to process what is needed within a second. By default, the room speed is set to 30 in every room. This means 30 steps are being processed every second, which in turn means the step event of any active instance is also being run 30 times every second.

# The draw event

Much like the step event, the draw event also runs every step of the game. The draw event is used to draw things to the game screen. This can be text, shapes, sprites, backgrounds, and more. Any time we want to draw something on the screen, the draw event is going to be used. This excludes sprites in most cases as GameMaker automatically draws sprites to the screen unless the draw event is being used in that object. If the draw event is in use, GameMaker allows the user full control over drawing and disables the automatic drawing of the instances sprite. The sprite must be manually drawn by the programmer.

There are also events for key presses, key releases, animation ends, rooms starting, collisions, and more. Events are the most basic building block of an object in GameMaker.

To see a complete list of all the available events in GameMaker, take a look at the online help file at http://docs.yoyogames.com/source/dadiospice/000_using%20gamemaker/events/index.html.

# Parents

In many other programming languages, it is possible to have objects created with the same attributes as another. In GameMaker, this is called parenting. A parent in GameMaker is any object that has had another object parented to it. Once an object has been parented, it can use the same code as its parent without it needing to be re-written. An object that has a parent is often referred to as a child object. Any events within the parent object are the ones inherited by the child, causing it to behave the same way. If an event is added directly to a child object, then the parent's event is discarded. It is, however, possible to still inherit the event using the GameMaker Language code.

# Making a parent

To make an object a parent in GameMaker, you actually need to open up the object that is going to be the child of that parent. In the object's properties on the left side, there is a button that says **Parent** on it.

By clicking on the blue options button to the right, a drop-down list will appear showing all the objects in your game for you to choose from. Choosing one of these objects will make it the parent of the object you are currently editing. Once a parent has been selected, you can click on the **Parent** button to open the parent object for editing.

# Parents and collisions

A very useful event in GameMaker is the collision event.

The collision event is triggered when the instance collides with another designated instance. A useful part of parenting objects is that all child objects of that parent will inherit the collision events defined within the parent object.

For example, you may have a number of different enemy objects — one that stands still, one that moves, and so on. Let's say you had a bullet that could kill all these enemies. For the bullet to collide with each different enemy object, it would need a separate collision event, for example, a collision event for the still enemy, a collision event for the moving enemy, and so on.

If we parent each enemy type to a single object, then we can make the bullet have a single collision event with that parent object. Due to the enemy objects being children of that object, the collision event is then applied to each of the enemy objects as well. The end result is the bullet having a single collision event with the parent object and all the children will be detected as well. This keeps things organized and easy to keep track of. One collision event is easier to manage than hundreds of them.

Parent objects allow us to group objects that are similar or that should function in much the same way.

# Depth

While working with objects in GameMaker, you may run into a few issues when it comes to one object going behind or in front of another. This is an issue caused by something called depth.

Depth in GameMaker is used to order objects from lowest to highest in a room. It can be seen much the same as a layer in an image editor such as Photoshop. By default, an object's depth is set to 0. If more than one object has the same depth value, then they will be ordered first to last, based on the order you create them in the room.

The higher an object's depth is, the lower it is drawn in a game room. So if an object with a depth value of one overlaps an object with a depth value of zero, then the object with the depth value of zero will appear on top of the object with a depth value of one.

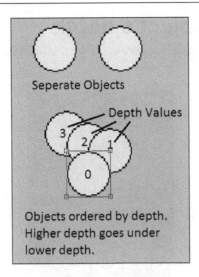

Seperate Objects

Depth Values

3 2 1

0

Objects ordered by depth.
Higher depth goes under
lower depth.

# Depth ordering

An object with a depth that is higher than another, will execute its code first.
Oftentimes, this greatly affects the creation of objects in a room. For example, a
button may need to appear on top of a character in the game when they overlap.
For this to happen, the character's depth value must be higher than the buttons.
This will mean that the character's draw event is run before the button's, which
will then result in the button being drawn on top of the character as desired.

Depth can be both the solution and cause of many problems when creating a game in
GameMaker. One of the most common issues seen is a variable not being recognized
within another object. For example, for a variable to be used, it must first be declared
at some point. So if we try to access a variable within another object before it has
been initialized, we will get an error. It is often seen that someone will initialize
a variable correctly in an object, and then have a different object trying to access
this variable and getting an error saying the variable does not exist. The reason
this happens is because the instance holding the variable is created after the other
instance, so when the other instance tries to access it, the variable does not yet exist.

All instances are updated separately within a game room. At every step, GameMaker
runs through each object and executes its code based on the object's depth in the
room. An object with a higher depth will be updated before an object with a lower
depth.

# Changing an object's depth

To change the depth of an object, open the object, and in its object properties, change
the **Depth** value.

# Drag and drop

One of the things GameMaker is well known for is the ability to create a game
without the need to actually program anything. This is done using the drag and
drop action in GameMaker.

A drag and drop action is essentially a piece of code that allows you to fill in the
blanks with a user-friendly interface. It makes it easy for even someone with no
programming knowledge at all to make a game.

To learn more about this, we are going to create a small game that will have the
player move an object around the screen. For this, we are going to be using events
and drag and drop actions.

We are going to need a new project for this. If GameMaker is not already open,
open it and go to the **New** tab on the start screen. Name the project `Drag and
Drop-Movement` and click on the **Create** button.

Once this is done, you will be presented with an empty project and we can get
started.

# Creating a sprite

To create sprites, perform the following steps:

1.  The first step we will be taking is to make a sprite so we can actually see our object move. To do this, click on the green Pac-Man-looking button on the main toolbar .


2.  This will show the sprite properties for the sprite you just created. Let's name the sprite `spr_player`. Notice the naming conventions mentioned in *Chapter 3*, *Resource Management* being used here.

3.  Now, click on the **Edit Sprite** button to open up the sprite editor. We need to create a new frame in this sprite to draw in. To do this, go to **File | New** and then set the **width** and **height** of the sprite to 32. It should already be this value by default.

4.  After doing that, we should have a blank frame in the sprite editor. Double-click on this frame to bring up the image editor where we can draw our sprite. With the sprite editor open, scroll on your mouse wheel or use the magnifying glass buttons on the top toolbar to zoom in.

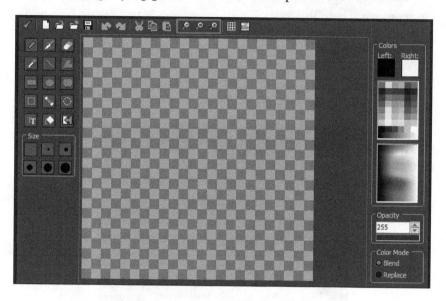

5.  Now, select the circle tool on the left and draw a circle from the top-left pixel to the bottom-right pixel. This will ensure our circle is the full 32 by 32 pixels in width and height.

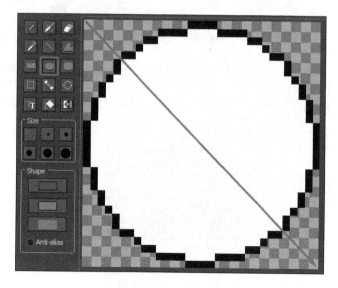

6. With this done, click on the green tick mark on the top left of the toolbar to save our frame. Click on the green tick mark on the frame viewer as well to save the whole sprite. The last thing we need to do is center this sprite's origin. To do this, click on the **Center** button in the sprite properties window. This will make the origin of this sprite the center point instead of the default top left.

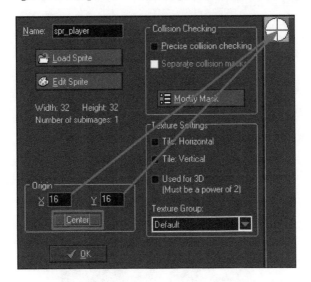

7. Click on **OK** in the sprite properties to save our changes. The sprite will now show in the resource tree under Sprites.

# Making our object

Next we need to make the actual object. To do this, create a new object by clicking on the green ball on the main toolbar.

This will create a new object and show its properties. Name the object `obj_player`. Once again, we use the three-letter naming convention. Next, we need to give this object our sprite by clicking on the blue button to the right of the box saying **<no sprite>**. Then, select the sprite from the drop-down list as shown in the following screenshot:

We are now ready to make our object move. We are going to give the player the ability to move the instance based on the keyboard buttons that are pressed.

For this, we need to add four events; keyboard left, right, up, and down, to our object. Click on **Add Event**. This will show the event window where we can choose which event we want to add.

On the event selection window, click on **Keyboard** and then on **<Left>**. This will add a new event to our object. This event will be triggered at every step while the key is being held down. This will allow us to move the object while the key is being pressed.

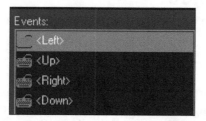

Add another event for **<Right>**, **<Up>**, and **<Down>** by repeating the process we mentioned earlier. We now have an event for each arrow key.

In the blank box to the right, we put our actions. Each event can have its own actions. Actions can be either drag and drop or code. In this case, we will be using drag and drop. To the right of the actions box, you can see a set of tabs. Each tab contains drag and drop actions allowing us to tell our object what to do during an event.

With the **<Left>** event selected, click on the **move** tab and drag in the first icon under **Jump**.

This will display a new dialog where we can tell our object where to jump. The purpose of this action is to move an object to an **x** and **y** position within the room.

In the dialog, enter -8 on the **x** axis, leave the **y** axis value at 0, and check the **Relative** option at the bottom of the dialog box.

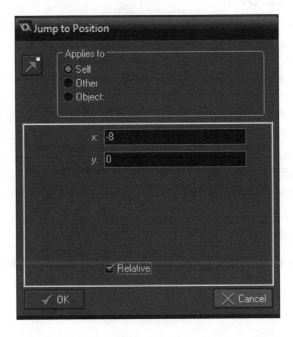

Before explaining the value, we need to know what the relative option does. The relative option makes the action work relative to the object's current values. If the relative option wasn't checked, this action would move our object to position -8 and 0, which is off to the left of the screen at the very top. This is due to the values being set directly. However, because we have **Relative** checked, the object will be moved eight pixels to the left.

It is important to note the way the axes work in GameMaker. On the **x** axis, right is positive and left is negative. So the further right the object is, the higher its **x** value. The further left the object is, the lower its **x** value. On the **y** axis, down is positive and up is negative. So the lower the object is, the higher its **y** value; the higher the object is, the lower its **y** value.

This is why we have entered -8 as our value for left as this will move our object left by taking eight away from its **x** value.

Now, we need to repeat the process on the other events. For the right event, enter 8 for the **x** value. For the down event, enter 8 for the **y** value. Finally, for the up event, enter -8 for its **y** value. Make sure the relative option is checked on every action.

To edit an action, just double-click on it in the actions box.

# Creating a room

The final thing we need to do is create a game room. To do this, click on the blank window button on the main toolbar .

This will create and show a new room. Click anywhere on the gray area within the room to place the object we have created. If there were more than one object, we could pick which one to place before selecting it from the object options on the left of the room editor.

With an object in place, we are ready to test our game. Make sure your compile target is set to **Windows** by looking at the **Target** option on the main toolbar. If it is set to something else, change it to **Windows** by clicking on the dropdown list.

Click on the green play button on the main toolbar to test the game once this is done .

When we run the game, you should be able to move the object around the room using the arrow keys.

# Summary

In this chapter, you learned about objects in GameMaker. You learned how they are structured and how they work in regard to events. You also learned how to use drag and drop options to make a simple game. We can now create objects, tell them what to do, and place them in a room to create a game.

Next, we will begin looking at GameMaker Language.

# The GameMaker Language

# 5

In this chapter, we will look at the GameMaker Language, or GML for short. You will learn how GML is structured in terms of its variables, functions, loops, and more. We will see exactly how each variable type is defined and created, as well as how to structure statements and loops correctly, allowing us to truly grasp the main concepts and features of GML.

## Variables

As in any programming language, the first things you should know is how to initialize different types of variables and how each variable type can be used. In GameMaker, there are four main types of variables: instance, local, global, and arrays.

### Instance variables

An instance variable is one that is local to the instance it is initialized in. This means that it is not directly accessible in any other instance within your game and must have the instance ID for it to be referenced from outside of the instance it is created in.

To initialize an instance variable, type its name, the equals sign (=), and then its value. The value can be either a real or a string. If the value is a string, then the text must be enclosed in quotation marks.

The following is a sample of two instance variables being initialized in GameMaker:

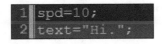

```
1  spd=10;
2  text="Hi.";
```

Once these variables have been initialized, they can be used in any event of the object.

# Local variables

A local variable is a variable that is local to the code block or script being run at the time of its creation. At the end of the code block or script it is created in, a local variable is automatically removed from memory.

As a local variable is not initialized in the create event, it must be initialized using the special function `var`.

The following is a sample of two local variables being initialized:

```
1  var spd=10;
2  var text="Hi.";
```

As you can see, the only difference between this and an instance variable is `var` in front of the variable name. Once a local variable has been initialized, it can be used throughout the rest of that code block or script. At the end of the code block or script, the variable will be deleted.

# Global variables

A global variable is a variable that can be used in every object in a GameMaker game from the point of its initialization.

To initialize a global variable, type `global.`, the variable name, the equals sign (=), and then its value, that is, either a real or a string.

The following is a sample of two global variables being initialized:

```
1  global.spd=10;
2  global.text="Hi.";
```

From the point of creation, the variables can be referenced by any object throughout the game, even in different rooms. The global variables are never removed from memory.

To reference the variables, you must type `global.` before the variable's name. If this is not done, you may receive an error stating that the variable does not exist.

# Macros

Macros are GameMaker's version of constants. A constant is much the same as a global variable except that its value may not be changed from the point of its creation.

Macros are most commonly used to store information such as an online scoreboard key or a commonly used filename.

To create a macro, go to the last branch on the resource tree that says **Macros**.

Open the branch by double-clicking on it, then double-click on **All configurations**.

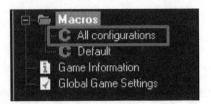

This will display the macros table for your current project. This table allows you to create, remove, and edit macros within your project. There will be two macros already created, **GM_build_date** and **GM_version**.

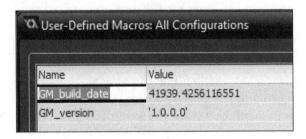

To create a new macro constant, click on the **Add** button at the bottom of the window, and then type the macro's name under the **Name** column and its value under the **Value** column. The value can be a string or a real.

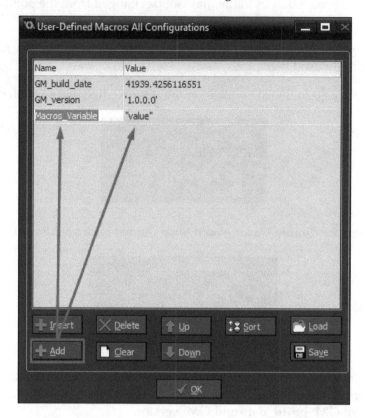

Click on the **Save** button and then on the **OK** button to save your macro.

This variable can now be used in any object in the game at any time. The variable should be syntax highlighted when using its name in code.

Syntax highlighting is the automatic highlighting of text when programming. For example, in GML, function names, resource names, and macro names are all automatically shown in a different color to the normal text. You can see this in the following screenshot:

```
//ini variabales
ini_open(INI);
global.sound=ini_read_real("data","sound",1);
global.music=ini_read_real("data","music",1);
global.difficulty=ini_read_real("data","difficulty",0)
```

As you can see in the preceding screenshot, function names are all shown in orange text and strings are shown in pink color. This is GameMaker's syntax highlighting at work. Syntax colors can be changed in GameMaker's preferences.

# Arrays

Arrays are like small tables that structure a number of values under one name. An array in GameMaker can be either one-dimensional or two-dimensional.

# One-dimensional arrays

A one-dimensional array is an array that holds data in one column.

To initialize a one-dimensional array, type its name, then an open square bracket, the index number, a closing square bracket, and then its value.

The following is a sample of a one-dimensional array being initialized:

If you want to create an array with multiple entries for a later time, simply put the index number as the number of entries you want to create. All entries will be created and set to zero by default.

To access the values, you must type the array name, as well as the index number enclosed by square brackets.

# Two-dimensional arrays

A two-dimensional array is an array that holds data in two columns.

Two-dimensional arrays allow for two index numbers to be used, meaning more data categorization within them.

To initialize a two-dimensional array; type its name, then an open square bracket, the first index number, a coma, the second index number, a closing square bracket, and then its value.

The following is a sample of a one-dimensional array being initialized:

The second index number can be seen as a second column in a spreadsheet. Two-dimensional arrays are often used for inventories, where entry 0,0 could be the string apples and 0,1 could be the number of apples the player has.

To access this information, you would type the array name, as well as the index numbers, for the value you wish to access.

# Functions

GameMaker Language is made up of functions. Functions allow for many things to be done, ranging from creating an object to drawing text to the screen. It is all done through the use of functions.

The basic structure of a function is, the function's name, an open bracket, function arguments, and a closing bracket.

```
function_name(arg1,arg2,arg3,ect);
```

An argument is a value that must be given to the functions in order for it to run correctly. As an example, let's look at drawing text to the screen.

To draw text to the screen, we will go to the draw event of an object and add a code block. In this, we will then type the function's name draw_text and a set of brackets directly after. Inside these brackets, we type our arguments.

To find out what arguments are needed, put the cursor in between the brackets and look down to the bottom of the code editor window. You will see the function name at the very bottom, and its arguments listed as shown in the following screenshot:

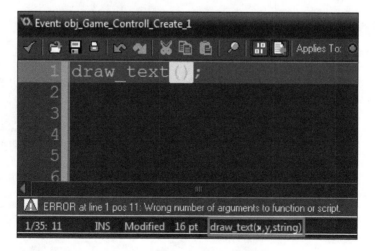

As you can see, we need to give it an **x** and **y** position, as well as a **string** to draw.

So, to draw text at the top left of the room, we will enter 0 for the *x* position and 0 for the *y* position. Arguments are separated by comers when typing them. For the string, we simply type any string we want to draw. Remember that a string is enclosed by quotation marks.

When running this code, it will draw our text to the top left of the screen.

All functions have the same structure but do different things. For a complete list of functions and what they do, open the GameMaker help file by pressing *F1*. You may also access documentation on a specific function by clicking on the scroll wheel of your mouse on the text or pressing *F12* with the text cursor somewhere within the function name.

The GameMaker help file can be seen online at `http://docs.yoyogames.com/source/dadiospice/`.

# Statements and loops

In nearly every programming language, there is the option to use statements such as `if` and `else`. Often, we need to use loops such as the `for` loop. Statements and loops make a programmer's life much easier when it comes to keeping code readable and organized, so let's take a look at how these look in GML.

Loops allow developers to greatly reduce the amount of code needed to execute a repetitive task. Instead of using multiple `if` statements, the programmer can summarize it all into a single loop, keeping the code short and concise.

# Statements

First, we will look at the simpler of the two statements. We will begin with the most commonly used statement, the `if` statement.

## The if statement

The `if` statement allows us to ask our game questions and then tell it what to do depending on the answer. The answer will either be true or false, never anything else.

In GameMaker, an `if` statement can be structured in multiple ways. An experienced programmer will often use brackets to enclose the functions or math used within an `if` statement; however, in GML, this is not needed. It is still recommended though if you plan to use other languages as it will help in learning languages structured the same way. GameMaker updates may also begin imposing these formatting rules.

Let's look at an actual `if` statement in GameMaker.

In the preceding screenshot, the code is checking to see whether one is greater than than two. Of course one is not greater than two, so this statement would return false as its result.

Based on the true or false result of an `if` statement, we then decide what to do. For example, we may destroy an object if its health is lower than a certain value. Code executed in accordance with an `if` statement should be enclosed in curly braces.

In the following screenshot, you can see the same statement but with a place for code to be executed:

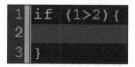

In between those curly braces, we will type the code to be executed if the statement was to return true. As the statement will return false, any code inside those curly braces will be skipped, and the program will move on to whatever is next.

## The else statement

What if we want to do something else when an `if` statement evaluates as false? For this, we have what is called the `else` statement. This allows us to do something when it evaluates as true; otherwise (if it does not evaluate as true), do something else.

The `else` statement must be accompanied by an `if` statement to work.

In the following screenshot, you can see how an `else` statement is structured:

As you can see, it is structured fairly similar to the `if` statement itself, the difference being it doesn't need something to check for it to function. Any code in the curly braces that follows the `else` statement will be executed if the `if` statement returns false instead of true. Should the `if` statement return true, then the code for the `else` statement would be skipped.

## The else if statement

What if we want to do something when the `if` statement returns false, but we only want to do it if something else returns true at the same time?

For this, we have the `else if` statement. If you guessed it being a combination of the `if` and `else` statements, then you are correct. The `else if` statement allows us to do something when the original `if` statement isn't true and another `if` statement is true.

That may be confusing, so let's look at an actual `else if` statement in use.

```
1 if (1>2){
2
3 }
4 else if (4>2){
5
6 }
```

In the previous screenshot, you can see the structure of an `else if` statement. As you can see, we start by saying `else` to the original `if` statement, and then follow with another `if` statement to check. In this case, the `if` statement following the `else` would be true as four is greater than two. Because the `else if` statement is true, the code inside the curly braces that follow would be executed.

## Loops

Loops are extremely useful when it comes to performing tasks such as checking large amounts of data or checking a function multiple times. GameMaker has four loops available for use. Let's start simple, shall we?

## The repeat loop

The simplest loop in GameMaker would have to be the `repeat` loop. The `repeat` loop does exactly what it says; it repeats.

The repeat loop will repeat any code in curly braces that follow it the number of times defined by the programmer. Here is a screenshot of how this looks:

```
1  var xx=0;
2  repeat (10){
3      instance_create(xx,y,obj);
4      xx+=32;
5  }
```

The code in the preceding screenshot is a bit more complex than the previous example, but what it does is simple.

It starts by initializing a local variable named xx. It sets this variable value to 0.

It then moves into the repeat statement. You can see number 10 in brackets to the right of it. This means the code within the curly braces will be repeated 10 times.

The first line in the curly braces creates a new object named obj at position xx,y in the room. Remember that xx is equal to 0 at the first run, so the final position is 0,y. y is a built-in variable that holds the object's current y position in the room.

The next line adds 32 to the xx variable. On first run, this would make xx equal to 32; on the second run xx would become 64, and so on.

The preceding code will create 10 objects in a line from left to right.

## The while loop

The while loop is a loop that repeats as long as a statement evaluates as true. This statement can be made of a function or an equation, and as long as the statement evaluates as true, the code in the curly braces that follow will be repeated.

This is a while loop in GML.

```
1  while (x<100){
2      x+=1;
3  }
```

As you can see, the while loop is structured much the same as an if statement. Except, instead of saying, if something is happening, do something, we are saying, while something is happening, do something.

In this case, we are saying while (x<100); add 1 to x.

As long as the statement returns true, the code will be repeated. If the object's x was equal to 0 before the `while` statement was run, then the code will repeat 100 times as one is added to x at every run.

Once x is over 100, the statement is no longer true and the loop stops.

It is important to be careful with this type of loop. If, for example, we accidentally typed x-=1 and we subtracted 1 from x at every run, your game would freeze until the operating system detects it as being unresponsive. This is what is called an infinite loop. An infinite loop is a loop that has no exit. It causes the game to loop through the one piece of code forever, and as this happens in the same step, the game will never progress any further.

# The for loop

The `for` loop is the most complicated but also one of the most commonly used loops. The `for` loop is often used to apply a change to many instances at once.

This is what a `for` loop looks like in GML:

```
1 for (i=0; i<10; i++){
2     array[i]=5;
3 }
```

Let's start by explaining what goes on in the `for` loop.

We start by writing `for` to define that this is a `for` loop. Next, we have a set of three essential parts to the loop.

1. `i=0;` sets a variable i to be equal to 0. This part has a semicolon at the end to define its end in the loop structure.

2. `i<10;` is our check. We check to see whether i is lower than 10. As it was set to 0 earlier, this is true. This part also has a semicolon at the end to define its end in the loop structure.

3. `i++:` ++ adds 1 to whatever variable is using it. In this case, it adds 1 to i. This part has no semicolon at the end; this is important. Adding one will cause an error in the game.

The preceding three steps are how all `for` loops are structured. However, any variable name can be used.

Basically, we set a variable to a number to start with. We then check to see if this number is equal, greater than, or lower than another number. Then, finally, we tell the loop what to do at the end. In this case, we add 1 to the variable and run the loop again if the variable is still lower than 10. You may also count down.

Whatever code is in the curly braces that follow will be executed every time the loop runs.

The preceding code sets an array's value to 5. You can see that no index number is used for the array and instead, we are using the i variable.

As i starts off being equal to zero, on the first run, the index number for the array is also 0. 1 is then added to i, making the index number equal to 1 in the second run, and so on through the rest of the loop.

This code goes through ten indexes of the array and sets the value to 5 for each of those indexes.

Once again, it is easy to make a for loop get stuck and freeze your game. Always be careful when using loops and make sure they have an exit before running your game.

# Scripts

Scripts in GameMaker are blocks of code not directly related to any object in a project. A script is accessible by all objects in a project at any time and allows developers to create their own functions using GML.

Scripts allow developers to create complex calculations and have the answer returned and stored in a variable as an end result. Scripts are also commonly used when multiple objects are meant to behave the same way. Instead of typing up the same code in every object, a script can be used and run in each object.

Let's take a look at scripts and how they are used.

# Creating a script

The first step to using a script is creating one. To do this, click on the icon in the main toolbar that looks a bit like a new page with a play button on it .

This will create a new script and display the code editor so we can start writing code. Before typing anything, we need to know what we want this script to do. Will it be a simple piece of code? Will it need to return a value at the end? How should we name this script so it is easy to understand? These are things we need to consider when it comes to creating a script.

# Naming a script

Let's start by naming the script. As an example, we will create a script that adds two numbers together and displays the result in a message. So, we can name our script `scr_Add`. Notice the naming convention used at the start, where `scr` is short for script.

# Writing a script

Writing a script is just like writing any other code. GML functions are the exact same in a script as they are in an object; the only difference is the script is global to all objects and not locked to any specific one. With this in mind, it is important not to accidentally try and use a variable from an object.

We want to add two numbers together and then display a message to the player with the answer. This can be done in one line of code; however, we will be extending it slightly to make it more readable, and also easier to edit later on.

This is the code we will use:

There are four lines of code in the preceding screenshot, each of which take the entire process one step at a time. Let's walk through these steps and see what's going on.

1. On line one, we create a new variable called n1. This variable is set to 5, and n1 stands for number one.

2. On line two, we repeat line one except with a variable called n2, which stands for number two. We set this variable to 10.

3.  On line three, we create another variable named `answer` and we set its value to be equal to `n1 + n2`, which would set this variable to 15. This is where our equation takes place.

4.  Finally, we show the result to the player using the `show_message` function.

# Executing a script

That's it for our script. It adds 5 and 10 together and shows a message. Now, we need to execute the script inside an object.

To do this, we go into an object and simply type the script's name followed by an opening and closing bracket as if it were any other function.

```
scr_add();
```

We can now run our game with the object in a room and we should see the following:

Those are the basics of using a script, but there are two more things that make scripts so powerful.

# Arguments in scripts

A script can have up to 16 arguments. An argument is a value or variable that is given to the script as it is run. This could be a number or a string.

Let's take a look at using arguments with our add script.

Instead of setting `n1` and `n2` to numbers directly, we are going to set them when the script is actually running through the use of arguments. To do this, we set `n1` to `argument0` and `n2` to `argument1`.

This is how our code should now look:

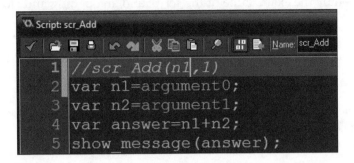

As you can see, we are no longer setting the variables directly to numbers and instead are giving them the value of arguments 0 and 1.

Now, how do we set what those arguments are equal to? To do this, we go back to where the script is executed in our object and input the arguments just like we would with any other function. We type their values in between the brackets separated by a comma.

The following screenshot shows how this looks in GameMaker:

As you can see in the preceding screenshot, this looks exactly the same as any of the built-in functions in GameMaker. However, this is a script we have created.

Run the game and you should get the exact same result as last time.

# Argument hints in scripts

In all the functions that are default to GameMaker, we are able to look to the bottom of the code editor to see exactly which arguments are required for the script to run. This is really helpful if you forget what arguments are needed. We can have this same hint message display for our scripts, as well.

To do this, create an empty line at the top of our script and type three forward slashes followed by the exact name of the script and an opening and closing bracket.

```
///scr_add()
```

We then type our hint message in between the brackets and separated by a comma.

```
///scr_add(n1,n2)
```

Hints should be kept as brief and simple as possible, but they can say whatever you like. In the preceding line of code, we are using n1 and n2 as this is a good reminder of what arguments to enter.

This is how the hint looks in GameMaker.

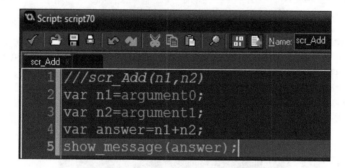

# Returning a value

The final part of a script is returning a value. This is done using the `return` function followed by the number, string, or variable you wish to return.

Being able to return a value from a script allows the script to be used completely like a normal function. We can execute a piece of code and then save the result in a variable for later use by the object.

Let's apply this to our add script. To do this, all we have to do is replace the `show_message` function with a `return` function, followed by the `answer` variable.

This is how it looks in GameMaker:

```
1 //scr_Add(n1,1)
2 var n1=argument0;
3 var n2=argument1;
4 var answer=n1+n2;
5 return answer;
```

That's it for our add script. We can now execute the script from within an object with any number we choose, and have the result returned and saved in a variable.

Let's go to our object and save this value to a variable, and then show a message with the result.

```
1 num=scr_Add(5,10);
2 show_message(num);
```

By typing num = scr_Add, we are saving the returned value to the num variable. We then display a message to the player, which will hold the value of num. If this works, it should show a message with the number 15 in it.

Feel free to experiment with different values to see how it works. Also, try creating a subtraction, multiplication, and division script for practice.

# Summary

In this chapter, you learned about the structure of GameMaker Language. You learned how to create variables and scripts as well as how to structure statements and loops. We can now use the scripts to create new functions within GameMaker that accept arguments and are able to return results for easy use.

In the next chapter, we will be working with sprites.

# 6
# Sprites

In this chapter, you will learn more about sprites. You will learn how to load a sprite into a project, how to edit the sprite's properties and change its options, how to size sprites to make positioning easier when designing levels, how to edit a sprite, and finally how to use GameMaker Language to change how the sprite plays and how it looks when drawn to the screen.

## Loading a sprite

Loading a sprite in GameMaker can be done in two ways:

1.  The first and most common way is to create a new sprite resource by clicking on the new sprite button , and then clicking on the **Load Sprite** button. This displays the default file browser, allowing you to find your sprite image file and open it as a sprite in GameMaker.

2.  The second way to load a sprite is by using your default file browser to locate the image file and then drag and drop it onto the GameMaker user interface. This will show a dialog asking what sort of resource you want it to be.

Clicking on **Sprite** will create a new sprite resource with the image file loaded as the sprite. Clicking on **Background** will create a new background resource with the image file loaded as the background. Clicking on **Included File** will add the image as an included file to the project.

An included file is a file that will be exported and packaged with your final project. This allows you to attach things such as text files, dynamic link libraries, or images to be loaded externally to the final project and have it all packaged together when the game is exported.

# Sprite options

There are many options related to sprites, some more commonly used than others, but all of them have their uses depending on the situation.

## Sprite origins

We will start with the most used option of any sprite, the origin.

The sprite origin defines the center point of a sprite. The origin is made up of two values, the **X** axis and the **Y** axis. The **X** and **Y** axes allow us to define the center point of a sprite on a 2D plane. A common place for a sprite origin is the middle of a circle, or the top left of a button.

The origin is represented by a gray cross on the image.

Sprite origin can be very useful when it comes to positioning and rotation. When placing an object in a room, the object locks to the grid based on the sprite origin attached to it. If the origin is in the middle of the object, then the object will look to the middle on the grid. When rotating a sprite, the origin is used as the pivot point. When creating something like a turret, you will put the origin on the place where you want the turret to rotate.

To change the origin of a sprite, double-click on the desired sprite to show its properties window. On the window, you will see a section labeled **Origin**.

Within the regions of this section, there are two boxes labeled **X** and **Y**. These show the **X** and **Y** positions of the sprite's origin. You can change these values to change the origin of the sprite. You can also click on **Center** to have GameMaker automatically find the center point of the sprite.

You may also change the sprite's origin by clicking and dragging anywhere on the sprite's preview image.

# Collision masks

GameMaker handles its collisions based on collision masks. A collision mask is a shape that is used to detect collisions with other objects. This can be anything from a simple square or circle shape to using the actual sprite as a mask.

GameMaker checks to see whether any point on a collision mask is overlapping another collision mask of a different object; if it is, GameMaker will perform a collision event for that situation.

A collision mask does not need to perfectly outline a sprite. The more basic a collision mask is, the faster the collision check can be performed, which in turn will optimize your game. Complicated collision masks can often cause problems when it comes to platform games or any other game that relies heavily on collisions. For a character animation, it is often best to have a simple rectangle collision mask that mostly covers the character animation. In most cases, a player will not notice the difference.

## Editing a collision mask

To edit a collision mask, start by opening the sprite properties for the sprite you wish to edit. Here, we can see a section of the options labeled **Collision Checking**:

This is where the editing of the collision mask starts. You can see two checkboxes, one labeled **Precise collision checking** and the other labeled **Separate collision masks**. **Separate collision masks** can only be used when **Precise collision checking** is enabled.

With **Precise collision checking** turned on, GameMaker will use the actual sprite as a collision mask. This makes collisions as precise as possible with the actual shape of the sprite being used. By default, this feature does not take alpha and transparency into account. Any pixel that has more than zero alpha on it will be included in the collision mask.

Below the checkboxes is a button labeled **Modify Mask**; clicking on this will show the mask properties window.

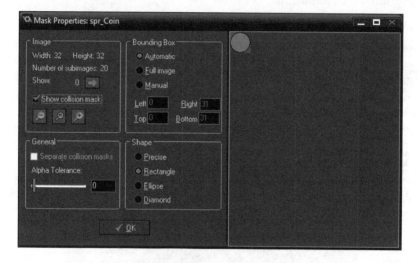

Here, you can see information about a collision mask as well as change its look. There are four main sections of control on this window.

The first is the **Image** control. Here, you can scroll through each subimage of an animation, toggle the collision mask display on and off, as well as zoom in and out on the image preview.

The next is the **General** control section. Here, you can toggle on separate collision masks and change the alpha tolerance, allowing pixels with low alpha to be left out of the collision mask.

The third section holds the **Bounding Box** options. Here, you can change the **Bounding Box** options, trimming off edges and changing the general settings. The **Left**, **Right**, **Top**, and **Bottom** input boxes allow you to enter how much to cut off in pixels.

The final section is the **Shape** section. Here, you can change the base shape of the collision mask. It is important to note that precise collision masks are extremely inefficient and should be avoided where possible to ensure a better frame rate.

# Texture settings

The final part of the main sprite options is the texture settings.

The first three settings of the **Texture Settings** section are based around 3D texturing in GameMaker. While GameMaker is focused on 2D game creation, 3D is still an option. In most cases, a background will be used to texture a 3D model in GameMaker. However, if you want to apply an animated texture, you will need to use a sprite.

The first two options are for tiling a texture either horizontally or vertically. Tiling a texture is the process of repeating the same image multiple times across the width or height of the model. This allows textures to be repeated across the surface of a model, meaning a small texture can cover a larger space without pixilation.

- **Tile: Horizontal** toggles the horizontal tiling of the sprite
- **Tile: Vertical** toggles the vertical tiling of the sprite

The final checkbox sets the sprite for use in 3D. This is not required to use the sprite in 3D; however, you may come across strange rendering options with it disabled, so it is always best to enable it if the sprite is to be used in a 3D environment.

The final option of the texture settings section is for setting the sprite's texture group. GameMaker allows for the creation of texture groups within projects. When GameMaker exports a project, all the project's graphics are saved into large images called texture pages. Every time GameMaker has to use a different texture page, it must unload the current page and load in the new one; this is called texture swapping and uses a small amount of CPU power, which can cause stuttering or slight freezes in larger games when not optimized.

Texture pages allow for graphic assets to be placed on a single texture page according to how the user groups them. This allows for menu graphics, for example, to be saved to a single page. Then, GameMaker does not need to do a texture swap during the menu, meaning no stuttering as a result. This can also be applied to separate themes or levels in a game. Texture groups allow for deeper optimization of projects.

Clicking on the texture group dropdown list will display all the texture groups currently active in your game. Select which group you would like to make the sprite a part of to add it to that group. You can define your own groups from **Global Game Settings**.

# Sprite sizing techniques

When it comes to level design, it is important to think about how big things are going to be. Will the game have small graphics and a small display size? Will it feature big graphics and have the camera pan to follow the player? These are things that should be thought about during the planning of any game.

This brings us to a not so big, but important issue when creating games.

Sizing techniques are used to scale and match graphics together so that everything fits within a game. We are going to take a look at some techniques that may help when creating graphics.

# The power of two

The simplest technique is the power of two. Keeping your graphics sizes to a power of two makes it easier to fit them on a grid; this is often important when it comes to keeping things symmetrical in a game. It also solves any issues with 3D texturing should the game feature such things. Due to the way graphics hardware works, powers of two are also more optimized. Common powers used are 8, 16, 32, 64, and 128.

# Templates

When it comes to making a lot of graphics that need to be of similar sizes or have similar looks, why not make a template? A template can be anything from an empty image of the correct size to a Photoshop file with layers set out and positioned correctly for icons or characters that need to be set up the same way. Templates are a great way to keep things looking right when creating graphics for a game. This especially comes in handy when creating multiple icons for each platform you are publishing your game to.

# Editing a sprite

Within GameMaker's sprite properties window, there is the option to edit the sprite.

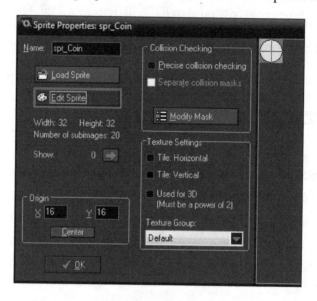

Let's take a look at this option in detail and see exactly what we can do here.

# Starting from scratch

Creating a sprite from scratch is simple. Start by clicking on the new sprite button on the main toolbar to create the new sprite and display its properties .

When the properties window is displayed, click on the **Edit Sprite** button to open up the Sprite Editor.

The Sprite Editor window is shown in the following screenshot:

It's very empty right now. This is because we currently have no sprite to display.

Let's create a new sprite. To do this, click on **File** and then on **New** in the top left of the window.

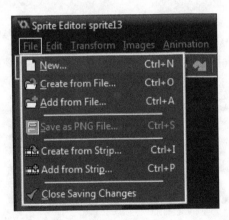

This will display a new dialog for us to enter the size of the sprite into. By default, this is 32 pixels in width and height. This is fine for this example, so just click on **OK** to create the new sprite.

Once **OK** is clicked, a new blank image should be shown in the subimage viewer.

A subimage is a single frame of a sprite animation. The sprite itself is the entire animation, whereas a subimage is a single frame of a sprite. The number associated with each sprite is its `image_index`.

We are now ready to draw something. Double-click on the subimage to open up the Image Editor.

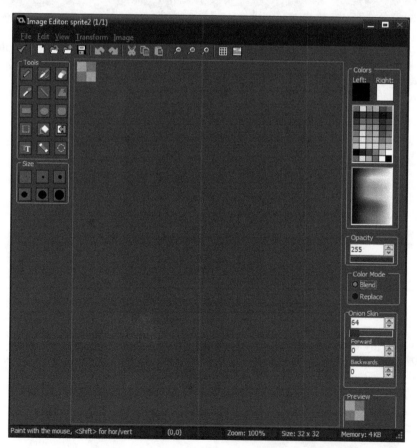

In the Image Editor, we can see our blank sprite as well as drawing tools, color tools, and some drop-down menus providing extra functions and basic effects.

Let's draw a simple circle.

To do this, select the circle tool from the left of the window and then click and drag from the top-left pixel to the bottom-right pixel on the blank sprite.

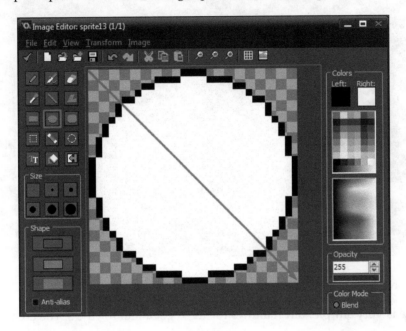

Zoom in by scrolling or using the magnifying glass icons on the main toolbar, if needed.

Now, select the paint bucket tool, pick a color, and fill the white circle with the new color.

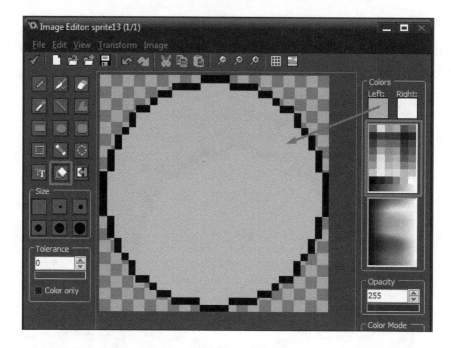

We now have a simple colored circle to use in a project.

This sprite is very simple, but it allows for us to get a feel for the sprite creation controls.

Click on the green tick ![tick] at the top left of the window to save the image and go back to the Sprite Editor.

The image will now show in the subimage viewer and we can use this sprite in our project.

# Effects

In the Sprite Editor, there are a number of effects that can be applied to our sprites. These can be found in the **Images** and **Animation** drop-down lists.

To see how some of these effects work, let's make our sprite shrink and change color while doing so. Then, to make the animation repeat smoothly, we will copy the animation and reverse it to make it return to its original state.

To start with, let's use the **Colorize** effect to make our image smoothly fade to a different color.

Click on **Colorize** under the **Animation** drop-down list.

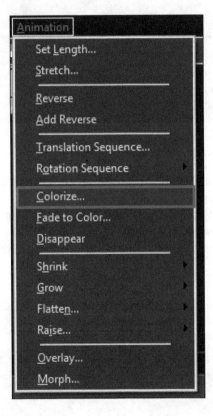

This will display the color selector. Use the slide bar to adjust the color of the image.

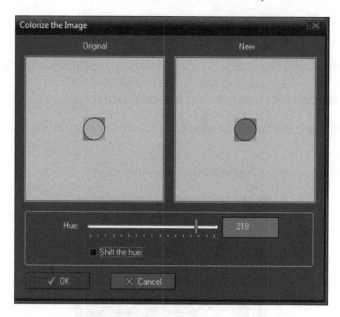

Click on **OK** once you have your desired color.

A new dialog will appear asking how many frames you want the animation to be. The more frames there are, the smoother the transition will look. However, more frames also mean a higher file size for the sprite. It is important to be aware of the file size of sprites as large file sizes are often something you want to avoid. Most of the time, large amounts of frames are unnecessary as the player will not notice the difference.

Enter 10 for the amount of frames to use and then click on **OK**.

You should now see the resulting animation in the Sprite Editor. To view a preview of the animation, toggle **Show Preview** to on.

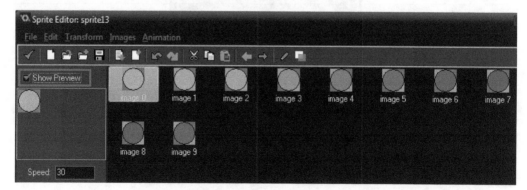

Now, we need to make the sprite shrink.

To do this, click on **Shrink** and then on **Center** under the **Animation** drop-down list.

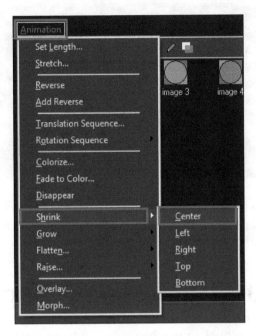

This will display another dialog box asking how many frames we want the animation to last for. It should show 10 by default. Leave the number of frames at 10 and click on **OK**.

The animation should now change color and shrink away to nothing.

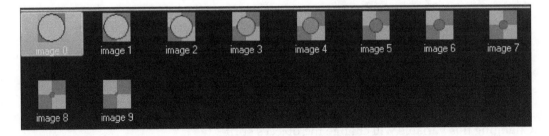

The final step is to make the animation repeat in reverse so that it smoothly goes back to its original state.

To do this, click on **Add Reverse** under the **Animation** drop-down list.

The result should be a smooth animation of a circle changing color and shrinking, and then changing back and growing to its original state.

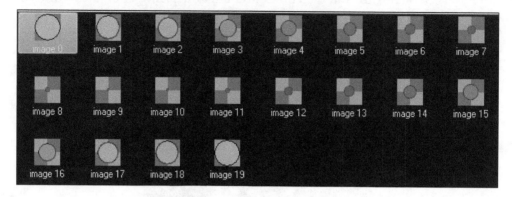

That is a simple example of some of the effects available in the Sprite Editor. However, there are many more to experiment with and use. Effects such as fade, grow, flatten, raise, and smooth edges are just a few that can be used.

# Sprites in the GameMaker Language

When it comes to making games with animation, it is extremely common for the animation to need to stop or change when an event happens. For example, the player pressing the right arrow key may make the game change the character's animation to a running animation.

You will learn to do this through programming using GameMaker Language in a new object.

Every object in GameMaker has a set of variables that allow users to control what sprite an object has linked to it, as well as the animation speed, current frame, and more.

# Setting an object's sprite

The `sprite_index` variable defines which sprite the object currently has set to it. Changing this variable will change the object's sprite.

The following is the example code:

```
sprite_index=spr_player;
```

# Getting the width and height of a sprite

The `sprite_width` and `sprite_height` variables return the width and height of the sprite currently linked to an object. This becomes useful when positioning text or other things around the sprite.

The following is the example code:

```
var sw=sprite_width;
var sh=sprite_height;
```

# Getting the offset of a sprite

The `sprite_xoffset` and `sprite_yoffset` variables return the $x$ and $y$ offset of a sprite. Offset is another word for the origin of a sprite. For example, if the origin of a sprite that is 32 pixels wide is centered, the $x$ offset will be 16 as that is half of 32.

The following is the example code:

```
var sxoff=sprite_xoffset;
var syoff=sprite_yoffset;
```

# Setting the animation speed of a sprite

The `image_speed` variable allows users to set the animation speed of a sprite. By default, this animation speed is set to `1`. The animation speed of a sprite is based off the room speed. If the image speed is set to `1` and the room speed is set to `30`, the animation will run through 30 frames every second.

The `image_speed` value is a multiplier, so to halve the animation speed, we will set it to `0.5`. This will mean, with a room speed of `30`, the animation will run through 15 frames per second as it takes two steps to run one frame.

The following is the example code:

```
image_speed=0.5;  //half speed
```

# Setting the frame of a sprite

The `image_index` variable holds the current frame number of an animation. The first frame of an animation has an index of zero with the other frames counting up in order from zero. An animation with 4 frames will have indexes from 0 to 3. The first frame will have an index of 0, the second with an index of 1, the third with an index of 2, and the fourth with an index of 3.

The following is the example code:

```
image_index=2;
```

# Setting the alpha of a sprite

The `image_alpha` variable allows users to set the transparency of a sprite. A value of one is not transparent at all, and a value of zero is completely transparent and in turn will seem invisible. However, this does not mean the sprite isn't being drawn to the screen. It is simply being drawn with zero transparency and is therefore still using memory resources.

The following is the example code:

```
Image_alpha=0.5; //half transparency
```

# Setting the rotation of a sprite

The `image_angle` variable allows users to set the rotation of a sprite in degrees. A higher number rotates the sprite in an anticlockwise direction.

A value of 0 would have the sprite with no rotation, a value of 90 would have the sprite rotated 90 degrees to the left, a value of 270 would have it rotated 270 degrees to the left, and so on.

The following is the example code:

```
image_angle=90; //pointing up
```

# Changing the scale of a sprite

The `image_xscale` and `image_yscale` of a sprite allow users to change the horizontal and vertical scale of a sprite. The default scale is a value of 1. Setting this higher will make the sprite bigger; setting it lower will make the sprite smaller. Setting the scale to a value lower than 1 will flip the sprite. For example, setting `image_xscale` to -1 will draw the sprite flipped to the left.

The following is the example code:

```
image_xscale=2; //double the size
image_yscale=2; //double the size
```

# Finding out how many subimages a sprite has

The `image_number` variable holds all the subimages a sprite has. This creates an easy way of making dynamic code that works even if you add or remove frames from a sprite.

The following is the example code:

```
image_index=image_number-1;   //sets the index to the last frame
```

# Summary

In this chapter, we took a detailed look at sprites. You learned how to change settings such as the sprite origin and the collision mask. You also learnt about sizing techniques and how they make it easier later on when building levels. Next, you learnt about editing sprites and made a simple animation using the built-in effects of the sprite editor. Finally, we took a look at the control variables of sprites and how they can be used to change an object sprite, set the animation speed, set the scale of a sprite, and more.

In the next chapter, we will create a simple game and put what you have learnt to practice.

# 7

# Making a Game

In this chapter, we will be creating our first actual game in GameMaker. The game will utilize most of the techniques and skills you learned in the previous chapters such as naming conventions and loops. We will be using a larger range of variables and `if` statements to create the user input and gameplay. There will be no drag and drop functions used in this chapter.

## Making the sprites

For this game, we are going to start by getting our sprites ready. We will keep things simple so we can move on to the actual game creation faster.

We need at least three sprites for this game. The first sprite we need is for the player's character, the second is for the player to collect and get points, and the final sprite is the wall that will keep the player inside the game view.

Let's create these now.

We will start off with the wall. Create a new sprite and make it a simple 32 x 32 black solid square. Name it `spr_Wall` and center its origin.

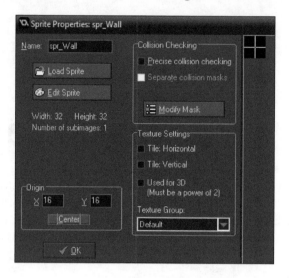

Next is the collect sprite. This sprite will be used for our collection object. The player's goal will be to collect these to earn points.

To keep things simple, we will just use another square sprite. We can change this later on if we want. Create another new sprite and make it a 16 x 16 yellow/gold square. Name it `spr_Collect` and center its origin.

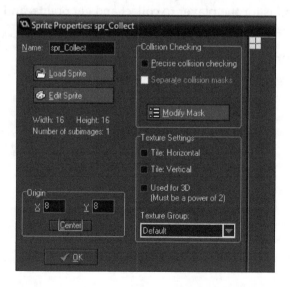

We will now make the player sprite. Once again, we will keep things simple and make another square. Create a new sprite and draw a 32 x 32 blue square. Name it `spr_Player` and center its origin.

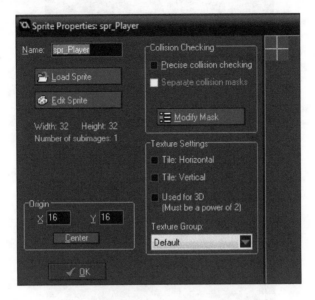

We now have the three essential sprites made and in the resource tree ready for use in objects.

# Room setup

With our sprites created, we are essentially ready to start making our objects, but first we need some place where we can actually place our objects. For this, we need a room.

Create a new room now. Go to the **settings** tab on the left side, and name the room
rm_Game.

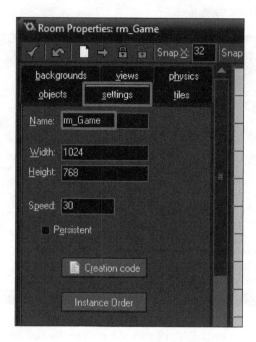

Here you can also change the dimensions of your room and in turn, your game.
Right now, the room size defines the total size your game will be on the screen when
it is not in full screen mode. You can change this by changing the **Width** and **Height**
values shown in the preceding screenshot.

If we were using a view, however, the game's size on the screen will be defined by
the view port. These options can be seen on the **views** tab directly above the **settings**
tab in the preceding screenshot.

# Views

In GameMaker, a view is a defined area of the screen that is viewable in the game window. These can be resized to create zoom effects or to make only a part of the room visible to the player at any one time. Views are commonly used to make a camera that follows the player through a level as they play. This limits the player's view of the entire level to only the amount defined by the developer.

# Object creation

With our sprites created and a room ready to go, we can now make our objects and program our game.

To start with, let's create the wall as there is no actual programming to make it work. Create a new object and name it obj_Wall. Link the wall sprite to the object, tick the solid option, and click on **OK** to close and save the new object.

At this point, we need to perform these steps for the collectable items. Create a new object and name it `obj_Collect`. Now, link the sprite to this new object and click on **OK** once again to save the object and make it ready for use.

Now, we will create the player object where we will do the programming and make the actual game. Create a new object and name it `obj_Player`. Then, give it the player sprite and we are ready to start programming.

# Programming the game

With our object created and ready to go, we are now also ready to program the game and make it work. All this will be done in the player object.

Add a **Create** event to the player object and then drag in a code block from the control tab on the right. You can actually change the default tab for objects in the GameMaker preferences.

The first thing we need to do is think about what variables we are going to need. We are going to make the game record the score, so we will need a variable for this. To make the code easier to edit, we can also create a variable for storing the maximum speed we want the player to move at. Finally, we can store our controls in variables to make the code easier to edit later on. The reason we store key controls in variables is so that if we want to change the controls later on, we can simply change the variable instead of changing every keyboard check.

Here is the code for our speed and control variables:

```
S=0; //score
max_spd=10;

key_right=vk_right; //move right
key_left=vk_left; //move left
key_down=vk_down; //move down
key_up=vk_up; //move up
```

The preceding code can be copied directly into your object if you wish; however, it is recommended to manually type it as that will help you to remember and understand what we are doing.

As you can see in the preceding code, we are simply initializing the variables we will need so they are ready to go. We will be using the key variables to check for keyboard presses in the step event and move our object.

The `max_spd` variable stores the maximum speed the object will be able to move in any direction. While we could type this directly into our code, this variable creates an easier way to change the speed of the object should we find it is too fast or slow.

We are now ready to program the movement code. Add a step event to our player object and drag in another code block.

To make our object move, we need to first check for user input on the keyboard. Remember, we have our controls stored in variables, so they can be easily changed.

For this, we are going to use an `if` statement. We need to use the `keyboard_check` function to check whether the keys are being held down and apply our changes should the statement return true.

This is the code for the left key:

```
if (keyboard_check(key_left)){
    x-=max_spd;
}
```

As you can see in the preceding code, we use our `key_left` variable as the argument telling the `keyboard_check` function which key we are looking for. So, the code is essentially asking the game whether the key stored in the `key_left` variable is being held down or not. If it is, we then subtract our `max_speed` variable from the object's current x position. This moves the object to the left as a result. If we add to the x position, the object will move right. We are now going to do this for the right key.

Re-type the `if` statement or copy and paste the entire code onto a new line. Then, change the `key_left` variable to `key_right` and change `x-=max_spd` to `x+=max_spd`. This will tell the game to move the object to the right if the key is being held down.

Our code now looks like this:

```
if (keyboard_check(key_left)){
    x-=max_spd;
}
if (keyboard_check(key_right)){
    x+=max_spd;
}
```

We can now move left and right, but what about up and down? We need to either re-write or copy the preceding code onto a new line below what we already have. Then, for the first `if` statement, we need to change `key_left` to `key_up` and `x-=max_spd` to `y-=max_spd`.

Now, for the second `if` statement, change `key_right` to `key_down` and `x+=max_spd` to `y+=max_spd`.

Our code should now look like this:

```
if (keyboard_check(key_left)){
    x-=max_spd;
}
if (keyboard_check(key_right)){
    x+=max_spd;
}
if (keyboard_check(key_up)){
    y-=max_spd;
}
if (keyboard_check(key_down)){
    y+=max_spd;
}
```

As you can see in the preceding code, we modified the third and fourth statement to change the y value instead of the x value. This is because left and right is done on the horizontal x axis and up and down is done on the vertical y axis.

We are now checking for every key and moving accordingly. If we put this into our room and run the game, we should be able to move the object around using the arrow keys.

Notice that if you are holding both the left and right or up and down arrow keys at the same time, the object will not move. This is because by holding down the left key, we subtract the `max_speed` variable from the x value moving us to the left, but immediately after, we then add our `max_speed` back to the x value, moving it back to the right. As this is done in one step, we don't physically see the change, although it does indeed happen. The reason we don't see the change is because, in this case, the screen is re-drawn at the end of each step and by that point, both movements have already taken place before the changes are displayed to the player.

Right now, if we place walls in our room, we will be able to move right through them. This is because we aren't telling the player what to do when in a collision or interacting with the walls in anyway.

To make it so, the player can't move through walls, we need to add a collision event with the wall and type some code to move the object back to its previous position.

In GameMaker, every object has a `xprevious` and `yprevious` variable built in. These variables are always holding the x and y position of the object from the previous step. If the instance has not moved between steps, then the previous values of x and y will remain the same.

Add a collision event with `obj_Wall`, drag in a code block, and then type in the following code:

```
x=xprevious;
y=yprevious;
```

What this does is when the player object picks up on a collision with a wall, it will set its x and y position back to its previous position, which is outside of the wall. This makes the player look like it has stopped when colliding with the wall.

Place wall objects around the border of the entire room and then run the game and try to move through them. If all has gone well, the player shouldn't be able to get out of the room.

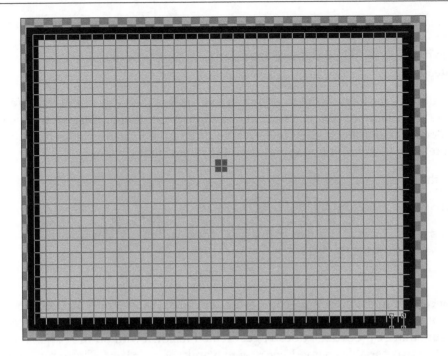

## Collectables

The next thing we need to do is make the collectable objects work. For this, we need to make the collectables spawn in the game room when none already exist. We will make them spawn in random positions. Then, we need to make it so the player is able to collect them and score points. The collectable then needs to be destroyed and a new one created in another place.

Let's start with creating the actual objects in the room.

To do this, we are going to use the player step event to check whether any collectable objects currently exist inside the room. If they do, we don't need to do anything; if not, then we need to create one at a random position.

For this, we will use the `instance_number` function. This function returns the number of instances you enter as an argument. In this case, we will be checking for `obj_Collect`. We want to check if there is less than one instance in the room.

This is the code we need to put beneath the movement code:

```
if (instance_number(obj_Collect)<1){

}
```

The preceding code checks the amount of `obj_collect` instances in the room to see if there is less than one. The `<1` controls the amount we are checking for. If we want to check to see whether there are more than five, for example, we will write `>5` instead.

We need to tell the game what to do when there is less than one object left. We want to create an instance of `obj_Collect` at a random position. For this, we will use the `instance_create` function that creates objects, and the `random_range` function, which returns a random number between the ranges that we set.

This is the code:

```
if (instance_number(obj_Collect)<1){

    instance_create(random_range(64,room_width-64),random_
range(64,room_height-64),obj_Collect);

}
```

As you can see in the preceding code, we use `random_range` for both the x and y arguments of the `instance_create` function. The reason we are using a range is to make sure that `obj_Collect` doesn't get created inside a wall on the edge. You may also notice two variables named `room_width` and `room_height`. These return the width and height of the current room in pixels. So, by entering `room_width-64`, we are simply entering a value that's 64 pixels back from the entire width of the room, which gives us our 64 pixel border.

There is one more thing we need to do before moving on. Due to values in a computer never being truly random, GameMaker uses what is called a **seed** to produce its numbers. This seed is always the same when testing the game, which means it will produce the same result in the same order every time the game is tested. To solve this, we can use the randomize function, which will randomize the seed that GameMaker uses.

In the create event of the player, we just need to put `randomize();` on a new line and the problem is solved.

We can now run our game and a single collectable object should be created.

Currently, the player still can't actually collect the objects, so let's fix that now. Add a collision event with `obj_Collect` and drag in a code block.

We want to make the game add one point to the score and destroy the collectable object. To do this, we will be using a `with` statement and a built-in variable called `other`. The `other` variable is one that holds the other instance's ID in it at all times. This can mean different things at different points in time. When we use it in the collision event, `other` will be equal to the instance's ID that we collide with. However, inside a `with` statement, the `other` variable will be equal to the object's ID that is executing the `with` statement.

The `with` statement is used to essentially go inside another object and execute code from that object. By inserting (`obj_Collect`), we are essentially telling the game to execute code from within that object instead of the current one. Within the brackets of the `with` statement, we are going to use the `instance_destroy` function to destroy the object we have collided with. If we didn't use the `with` statement, then the `instance_destroy` function will destroy the player object.

Here is the code:

```
with (other){
    instance_destroy();
}
```

The first line in the preceding code basically tells GameMaker to start executing code from within the object we have collided with. The `other` variable holds the ID of the instance we collided with at this point.

In between the brackets, we use `instance_destroy` to destroy the instance. This means that we destroy the collectable object that we collided with.

If we run the game now, we should be able to move around the screen and collect the collectable objects. A new object should be created every time we collect one.

Now, we need to tell the game to give us a point every time we collect an object. Inside the collision event with `obj_Collect`, go to a new line and enter `s++;`. Remember that `++` means plus one. This will add one point to our score variable.

Right now, the player can't actually see the score, so we need to draw it to the screen for them to see. To do this, add a **Draw GUI** event under the **Draw** section.

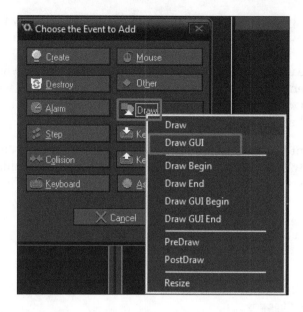

The **Draw GUI** event draws to the GUI layer of the screen. The GUI layer is drawn after everything else on the screen, which means it will always be on top. Therefore, other instances won't overlap or go on top of the text that we've drawn unless they too have a draw GUI event and lower depth value. The GUI layer is also independent of views, which means, even if a view moves, everything drawn to the GUI layer will appear in the same position on the screen.

We are going to use the `draw_text` function to draw text to the screen. We are also going to use the `string` function to convert our score variable into a string so we can add it to the text we've drawn.

Here is the code:

```
draw_text(64,64,"Score: "+string(S));
```

We start off with the function's name, `draw_text`. Next, we have our x and y positions from where we want to draw the text on the GUI layer. For this, set 64 on the x axis and 64 on the y axis; this will put the text in the top left of the screen but, will not overlap the wall objects.

Then, we enter the string we want to draw. This requires some explanation. All strings must be enclosed with quotation marks. This is why we have `Score:` in quotes in the text. We need to put a space after the colon so the score's value is spaced out by one. Anything inside of the quotes will be drawn to the screen including spaces. Next, we are using the `string` function to convert our score variable to a string and add it to the manually entered string. Eventually, we end up drawing in the following format:

```
Score: <value>
```

If we run the game now, we should see the score being drawn to the top left of the screen and the value should rise every time we collect an object.

# Enemies

We now have the very basics of a game. We have a player who has something to do. However, there is no challenge to the game at this point. In nearly every game, there is some sort of challenge or problem to overcome. This gives the player more purpose and makes their goal harder to achieve.

For this game, let's simply add in some enemies. These enemies will spawn randomly just like the collectable items, and they will also randomly choose to go either vertically or horizontally. When they collide with a wall, they will turn around and go the other way. We can also randomize their speed to add more variety and challenge.

Once again, let's start by creating a new sprite. Name it `spr_Enemy` and create a simple 32 x 32 red square. Once again, this can be changed later on, but for now, let's keep things simple.

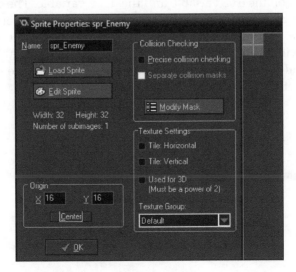

Now, create a new object and name it `obj_Enemy`. Link the new sprite to it; then, add a create event and drag in a code block.

There are three essential variables we need to create for this object: one to control the speed, another to control the direction it moves in, and one more to control its up/down or left/right state. Let's name them `spd`, `dir`, and `dir2`. We are going to use the choose function on the `dir` variable and the `dir2` variable. The choose function will randomly pick between a set of 16 or less arguments that we enter. In this case, for the `dir` variable, we will enter two arguments; `0` and `1`. `0` will mean horizontal movement and `1` will mean vertical movement. For the `dir2` variable, we will enter `-1` and `1` for left and right, respectively. For the speed variable, we will use the `random_range` function again and put in a range of `1` to `8`.

Here is our create event code:

```
spd=random_range(1,8);
dir=choose(0,1);
dir2=choose(-1,1);
```

Now, we need to add a step event. Here, we will control the object's movement based on the three variables we just initialized in the create event.

To start with, we need to check which direction the object is meant to move in. We do this using an `if` statement to check the `dir` variable. If it is equal to 0, we execute our horizontal movement code; if it is equal to 1, we execute our vertical movement code.

For the actual movement, we will be using `dir2` to decide whether we should be moving left, right, up, or down.

For this, we are going to use some simple math. Instead of having an `if` statement check the value and add or subtract from the object's x value, respectively, we can shorten and optimize our code just by adding to the x value.

By adding our speed variable multiplied by `dir2`, the object will move left and right according to the `dir2` variable. This works because multiplying a value by 1 simply equals the original value, but multiplying a value by a -1 equals negative the original number. When we add a negative number to the x value of an object, we actually end up subtracting from the x value. So, while `dir2` is equal to 1, the object will move right; and then when `dir2` is equal to -1, the object will move left.

This is our step event code:

```
if (dir=0){ //horizontal
    x+=spd*dir2;
}
if (dir=1){ //verticle
    y+=spd*dir2;
}
```

As you can see, vertical is the same as horizontal, except we edit the y value of the object instead of the x value.

The last thing we need to do is make the enemy change directions when it collides with a wall. Add a collision event with the wall object and drag in a code block.

The direction of the enemy is controlled by the `dir2` variable, so all we have to do to make it turn around is multiply `dir2` by -1. This way, if `dir2` is equal to 1, it will be set to -1 and vice versa.

Here is the code:

```
dir2*=-1;
```

The second to last thing we need to do is make it so that colliding with an enemy will end the game. There are many ways this can be done. You can take the player to a new game over room, display some sort of overlay, or more. To keep things simple, we will just show a message telling the player their score and restart the game.

Open the player object and add a collision event with the enemy object.

To display a message, we can use the show_message function. In here, we type a game over message and add the score in by simply using the plus symbol to add in the score variable converted to a string using the string function.

Then, we can use the game_restart function to restart the game.

Here is the code:

```
show_message("You died! Your score was "+string(S));
game_restart();
```

The final thing to do is make the enemies spawn. To do this, bring up the player object and then open the code in the collision event with obj_collect. Now, on a new line, we will use the instance_create and random_range functions to create a new enemy object just like we did in the step event of the player to create collectables.

Here is the code:

```
S++;
with (other){
    instance_destroy();
}
instance_create(random_range(64,room_width-64),
   random_range(64,room_height-64),obj_Enemy);
```

That's it. If we test the game now, we should have a moveable player, collectable objects, and enemies that spawn and move randomly when we collect an object. If we collide with an enemy, our score should be shown in a game over message and the game should restart.

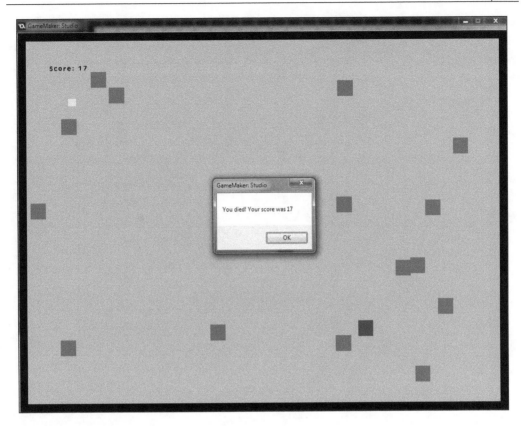

Feel free to experiment and add to what we have already created. Change the graphics, adjust the controls, or maybe add more features. Learning to make games is all about experimenting with the tools we have available.

# Summary

In this chapter, we created our first simple game in GameMaker. We used the GameMaker Language to program our game with variables, functions, and statements. We pieced together a functioning game using objects and sprites, and we can now build off what we have already made to improve and learn from it.

In the next chapter, you will learn about debugging a game in GameMaker.

# 8
# Debugging

In this chapter, we will look at the process of debugging. As with any engine or programming language, it's easy to end up with bugs in your code or things that just plain don't work. This happens to all game developers no matter their skill, so it's important to be able to debug these errors or problems and solve them as fast as possible. In this chapter, we will look at a few techniques on debugging of games and also how to read common errors in GameMaker.

## Errors

We will start with common errors in GameMaker. Things such as undeclared variables or non-existent objects will cause GameMaker to produce an error (stating basic information of what went wrong and where in the code it happened). There is no single cause for this, so we will look at a few common errors that may occur and see how to read them in order to get closer to finding the problem.

# Undeclared variable

The following is a screenshot of an error produced by an undeclared variable:

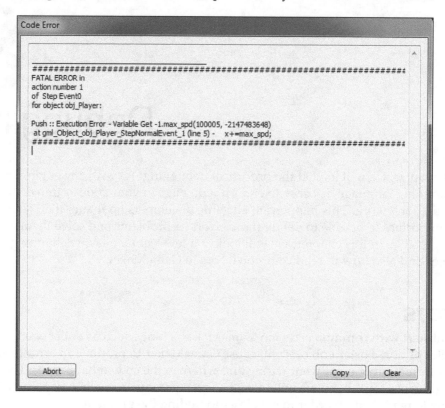

All GameMaker errors look similar to this one. However, depending on the problem, there may be more or less information provided regarding the error.

Here is an image of just the text so that we can better read what is going on:

```
###############################################
FATAL ERROR in
action number 1
of Step Event0
for object obj_Player:

Push :: Execution Error - Variable Get -1.max_spd(100005, -2147483648)
 at gml_Object_obj_Player_StepNormalEvent_1 (line 5) -   x+=max_spd;
###############################################
```

You will probably notice the lines of hashtags; these are more or less just borders or line breaks. Feel free to ignore them.

The first four lines are important; they show exactly where and in which object the error took place. As you can see, the error states that in **action number 1** and **Step Event0**, the error took place. It also states that the error took place in object **obj_Player**. This accurately shows us exactly where the error actually took place. So, based on this, we will go to our obj_Player object and then go to **action number 1** in the step event.

From this point, we can start checking the code for issues, but instead of aimlessly searching through code, there is more information we can gather from the error message.

In the next set of lines, there is a bunch of seemingly random information at first glance. In the first line, we can see **Push :: Execution Error - Variable Get -1.max_spd**. This line alone states exactly what is going wrong. **Variable Get** essentially means that the variable the program was trying to access does not exist or the program simply can't find it in memory. The error also states the actual variable it was searching for by entering **1.max_spd**. This means the **max_spd** variable can't be found.

We now know exactly what variable had the issue. Once again, though, we don't know where in the code there was an issue and also what the program was trying to do at that time. However, this information can also be found in the error produced.

In the final line, we can see **gml_Object_obj_Player_StepNormalEvent_1**. This essentially states that the error took place in obj_Player in the normal step event. The line then continues with **(line 5) - x+=mac_spd**. This means the error took place in line five of the code block and that the code GameMaker was trying to execute is x+=max_spd.

We now know not only what object and event the error took place in, but also in what line of code and what code was being executed. We can see all this before even closing the game.

At this point, it's now completely dependent on how you have programmed the game as to what the fix is. Here are some common causes of an unfound variable:

- The variable has not been declared (create event, global variable in another object, and so on)
- The variable was misspelled either on declaration or in that line of code
- The variable is being declared after that line of code (often declaration happens in another object)

By understanding errors, it becomes much easier to see where the problem is and how to fix it. No error is normally the same as another. You may cause more errors by fixing another. It is completely dependent on the game being made. GameMaker also has information about each of the possible compiler error messages in the debugging section.

# Drawing information

When it comes to debugging a game, it can often be helpful to draw information to the screen. Things (such as drawing variable values) can be extremely helpful in seeing exactly what is going on in the game at any one time.

# Drawing text

As mentioned before, drawing text to the screen can be extremely helpful. While prototyping parts of a game, such as a health system, you could simply draw the health value in text instead of going straight to a health bar.

It's common to see counters when using text to debug games. If we want to check how many of an object exists at any one time, we can draw the number to the screen using the `draw_text` and `instance_number` functions. This allows you to see exactly how many instances of an object exist when the game runs.

We can use text to see pretty much anything during a game. Things such as the position of an object to the text the user has entered on the keyboard can all be seen by simply drawing variables to the screen as the game runs.

There is a `show_debug_message` function that will display a message in the debug console when it's executed. This allows you to review the messages displayed at your own pace.

# Drawing lines and shapes

The second most useful thing to draw to the screen is a line or a shape. This allows you to see things that aren't naturally visible to the player via a sprite or background.

A common use of drawing a shape is when you see a circle around an object showing the range of that certain object. This is common in tower defense games. In GameMaker, we can do the exact same thing by using the `draw_circle` function and a range variable to set the circle's radius.

Circles, rectangles, and other shapes can also be used to draw basic objects. For example, if we were making a system for later use and didn't want to use sprites, we could just use the draw functions to show basic representations on the screen.

Lines can be used to show where a player is aiming. For example, when the mouse is used to aim a gun, you can draw a line from the gun to the mouse to act like a laser. This allows the player to be more accurate with their shooting.

# Simple toggles

When debugging a game, it's often useful to be able to enable or disable things with the press of a button. Things such as lasers, turrets, and pausing the game can all be done with just the press of a button and a single line of code.

For this, we will use the not statement, which is also represented by an exclamation mark (!). The not statement is often used in an if statement to check whether something is false instead of true. The way it works is by simply multiplying the returned result by -1, making it negative if the number was positive or positive if the number was negative.

We can use this to create toggles. Here is some example code:

```
if (keyboard_check_released(vk_space)){
    on= !on;
}
```

The preceding code checks to see whether the player has released the *spacebar* key and if so, it will set the on variable to be the opposite of what it was before. This works by setting on to !on. In other words, by multiplying on with -1.

This code will work the exact same way:

```
if (keyboard_check_released(vk_space)){
    on*=-1;
}
```

These toggles can be applied to anything that needs a variable to turn on and off. They become extremely useful when debugging a game as they allow the programmer to enable and disable parts of the game at any time and see exactly where the issues are taking place.

# The GameMaker debugger

GameMaker actually has a debugger built into it that runs alongside the game as it's being tested. To run a game in debug mode, click on the red test play button instead of the green one .

When running the game in this mode, the game will start as normal. The difference is that the GameMaker debugger will also start and automatically connect to your game.

The debugger will look something like this:

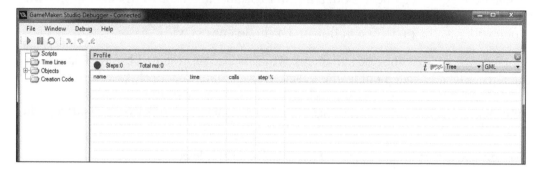

Using the debugger window, we can see pretty much everything the game is doing.

We can also see the source code of the game when it runs and add break points on the fly. A break point is a point where the game will pause on a certain line. These are often seen, for example, after medium to large changes during a game so that the programmer can see the result clearly. We can have the game step through the code and watch as each line is executed.

If the source code is not already showing, click on the gray close button at the top-right corner of the current form to close it .

Then, right-click anywhere on the now blank screen and choose **Source** from the drop-down list that appears. With the source form open, you should now see some source code from the game that is running:

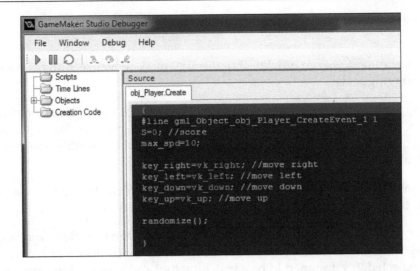

From this window, we can see all the source code for our game. To go to different sections of code, use the tree structure on the left-hand side of the debugger window to select objects, events, or scripts you wish to see.

To add a break point, double-click on the line. A red dot should appear to the left of the line when a break point is active. To remove the break point, double-click on the same line again.

When the game reaches this line of code, it should automatically pause.

To see the code line by line, we need to start by pausing the game if it's not already paused by a break point. Do this by clicking on the green pause symbol at the top-left corner of the debugger window ▉▉.

This will pause the game in its current step, and we can then use the step controls at the top of the debugger window to control what the game does ▨▨▨.

The first button is the step in button. This button steps into a code block.

The middle button is the step over button. This button steps over a code block and skips it.

The last button is the step out button. This button steps out of a code block and ends it.

Using these buttons, we can quickly skip through or skip over sections of code to make debugging easier.

The debugger has a large number of things we can watch. To see them all, simply close the form using the gray close button and then right-click on the empty space to open a new form. We can see things such as all the global variables currently declared, all the instances currently active, and so on.

Some forms require the game to be paused to display information, so if a form shows up blank, try pausing the game using the green pause button.

The debugger is an extremely useful tool, which allows you to watch every aspect of a GameMaker game as it runs and will come in handy when things aren't working quite as expected. It's designed to be a watching tool and provide information on your game. The game cannot actually be edited in real time as it runs, so all changes will need to be made in GameMaker itself.

# Summary

In this chapter, you learned how to debug games. You also learned how to read a general GameMaker error, how drawing to the screen can help solve problems, how toggles can be made to control the game easily, and also about the GameMaker debugger.

In the next chapter, you will learn about game settings and how to export your game as a final product.

# Game Settings and Exporting

In this chapter, we will take a look at GameMaker's Global Game Settings, where we can change our games icon, display name, project name, and so on. We will then take a look at game advertising and analytics, which allows us to track how many people play our game and also earn a small amount of revenue through advertising. We will also export our game as a final product when we have our settings ready so we can share it with the world.

## Global Game Settings

Every project in GameMaker has its own global settings. These settings include things for every export module, including Windows, Android, iOS, Linux, and so on. Things such as general options for texture groups and project information can all be changed in the Global Game Settings.

To open the Global Game Settings, double-click on the very last item on the resource tree that says **Global Game Settings**:

The **Global Game Settings** should then open, showing the **General** game settings tab:

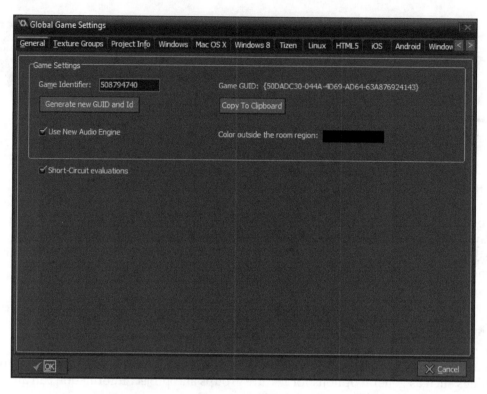

From this tab, we can change the Game ID, which is a unique key code used to identify the game. We can also toggle on and off the **Use New Audio Engine** as well as **Short-Circuit evaluations**.

The new audio engine is a completely new engine introduced in GameMaker: Studio. It allows for positional audio and is much faster than the old engine.

**Short-Circuit evaluations** are used to make GameMaker leave an `if` statement as soon as something returns false. If we check multiple cases in a single `if` statement, then one of them may return false. In previous versions of GameMaker, the `if` statement would continue to run every check even if a previous one had already returned false. Short-Circuit evaluations make the `if` statement stop as soon as a case returns false.

From here, we can also change the color that will show outside the visible region of the game. For example, if the game is scaled to fit the view, some letterboxing may be applied to keep the aspect ratio. This option controls the color of this letterboxing.

When you look at the top of the window, you can see a list of tabs, most of which are labeled based on the export module they are related to. Clicking on these tabs will take you to the respective options to export to this module.

The two arrows to the right of the tabs are for scrolling through each tab. Scrolling across reveals more options depending on the license modules you have.

Options such as **Analytics** and **Advertising** are being made obsolete as YoYo Games updates GameMaker: Studio. These services are now being provided through the use of extensions, so feel free to ignore these tabs.

Let's take a look at some export settings for the Windows platform. Click on the **Windows** tab to bring up the options:

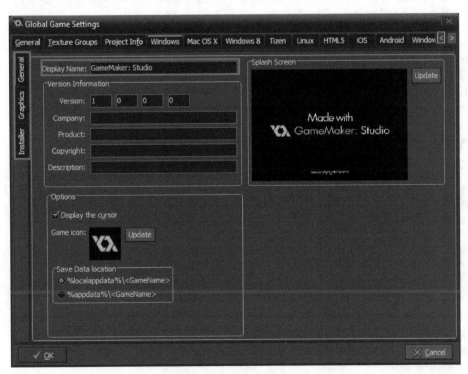

In this tab, we can change all the main aspects of the final game that will be compiled and exported. From the first set of options, we can set the display name, change the version information, and change the game icon and default save location of the game's files. We also have the option to change the splash screen, which is displayed as the game does its initial loading. This doesn't normally take long.

On the left-hand side, we have three other tabs that categorize and further extend the options for the export module. The second tab is for **Graphics**. Here, we can set the default graphics options for the game. We can choose to have the game start in full screen mode, allow the player to resize the window, change the texture page size, and so on.

The third set of options is for the **Installer** of the game. When exporting the game with the Windows module, we actually have three export options. The default is to export with the game packaged into a game installer. These options allow us to change the look of the installer, change the way the installer behaves, and also change the license agreement of the installer.

Another option is to export the game into a standalone application. This is a single executable file that runs on its own without external files.

The final option is to export the game into a compressed zip file. Doing this will export the game files into a single compressed zip folder.

Each tab related to export modules has different options. For the most part, the **General** tab is all about the game (general information such as its display name, version number, as well as other general settings and options available for this module).

# Analytics and advertising

When it comes to creating games, a lot of developers wish to make some sort of money from their work. Not only do they want to create a unique experience that the player enjoys, but they also want to see some sort of reward for their work, most commonly in the form of revenue.

While simply selling a game can work, it isn't always the best way to go about the process of making money, especially on mobile. Most developers don't just want to give their games away for free as they have put hard work into the game; therefore, it has value. This is where advertising comes in. Placing advertisements in our games allows us to generate a small amount of revenue as the ads are displayed to players. The greater the number of people playing the game, the greater is the revenue generated. This way, a popular app or game can still see a decent return in revenue over time.

Analytics are essentially stats. They allow developers to see how their app is performing and how people are using their app. Not only do analytics provide numbers or information regarding players at any one time, including which country most players reside in, but they also allow us to specify events within the games code. Google Analytics is a great example of this. By placing analytics events in our project, we can see exactly what the players are doing within the game.

Let's take a look at how these systems can be implemented in our project. For this, we will use AdMob and Google Analytics as our services. Other services are available to use and no service will be exactly the same; however, most will be similar. These services will be implemented for an Android application.

Analytics and advertising are not available on desktop export modules (Windows, Mac, Linux) and are mainly mobile only.

# Advertising

When it comes to advertisements, we nearly always have to start by adding a new app to our choice of service. Even before the app is released, we need to set up a new app listing on the service. This way, we can get our application ID and have ads sent to the app as needed.

We are using AdMob as our advertising service. The website can be reached by going to `https://www.admob.com`.

We need an account to be able to start adding apps. So, click on the register button located at the top-right corner of the web page and follow the on screen instructions to set up a new account. If you already have an account, simply log in. As Google services are able to use the same Google accounts, we should use the same account for both AdMob and Google Analytics to keep things organized and easy to manage.

Once a new account is made, log in and we are ready to add our new app listing.

There should be a **Monetize new app** button on the page that looks similar to this:

Click on this button to create a new app listing. From here, follow the on screen instructions to add your new app listing to AdMob. At some point during the process, there will be a section to create an ad. When selecting the type of ad to display, select **interstitial**. This is a full screen ad and we are using this as they are the simplest type to add to our game.

Once the listing is created, we should end up at a page where we can see the app listing and also a single ad unit that should be added during the app listing creation process:

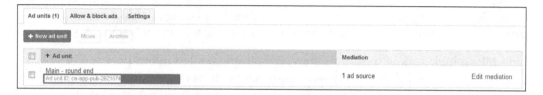

Beneath the ad name, there will be an ID code, which we will need to be able to display ads in our game.

We now need to open GameMaker. As ad services are now run through the use of extensions, we need to get the AdMob extension. To do this, open GameMaker and go to the **Demos** tab on the welcome screen. Open the **Ad Providers** section on the tree listing and select the **Google_Mobile_Ads** project. Then, click on the **Create** button. There may be a prompt to download the project; if so, download the project to open it.

Once the project is open, there should be multiple resources available to open in the resource tree. Feel free to browse these as they provide explanations on how to use the extension.

Open the **Extensions** section of the resource tree and we will see an extension called **GoogleMobileAdsExt**:

Right-click on this listing and then select the **Export Extension** option from the drop-down list. This will bring up Windows Explorer, which allows us to select where to save the extensions. Save the extension somewhere it will be remembered as we need to import this extension into our own project.

Once this is done, we are ready to go. Open either a project of your own or the one created during *Chapter 7, Making a Game*.

We now need to import the extension into our own project. To do this, right-click on the extensions listing in the resource tree and select **Import Extension**. Then, browse to the location where the exported extension is saved and load it into this project.

The extension should now show inside our resource tree. Open the extension in the resource tree to reveal the functions available to us.

The first thing we need to do is initialize the extension. This should be done before any other ad function is used. In the project created in *Chapter 7, Making a Game*, this should be done in the player object's create event. Add the GoogleMobileAds_Init function to a new line in the create event.

We now need the ad ID code that we saw on the AdMob web page. Copy the code and paste it in between quotation marks as the argument for the GoogleMobileAds_ Init function:

```
ca-app-pub-2902099209220920/9999091909
```

We can now display ads in our game. All we need to do is load an ad and then display it. Ad loading times vary depending on the Internet connection of the player.

Let's begin loading an ad right away. On another new line in the create event of the player, add the `GoogleMobileAds_LoadInterstitial` function by loading the ad as early as possible. This means the ad has more time to load before actually being shown.

We are going to display the ad when the player dies, so in the collision event with the enemy object, we need to add a new line before the `game_restart` function and then type the `GoogleMobileAds_ShowInterstitial` function. To load a new ad, simply use the `GoogleMobileAds_LoadInterstitial` function again after displaying the ad.

Now, when the game starts, the ad extension is initialized and we begin loading an interstitial ad. When the player dies, as long as an ad has loaded, it will be displayed to the user. Export the game as an Android application and install it on any Android phone or tablet to test the ads.

Ad revenue varies for each service; in order to find out how much you are earning, visit the AdMob website.

# Analytics

Analytics allows developers to get an insight into how people are using their application, as well as how many people are using it and where these people are from. Analytics allows us to monitor a number of stats regarding the use of an application, allowing us to improve the application if we find something wrong.

Setting up analytics for a game is a simple process and starts out much the same as setting up advertisements. For this example, we will use Google Analytics.

To start with, we need a Google account to link our Analytics account to. It is advised to use the same account as we did for AdMob so things are organized and easy to remember.

Go to `http://www.google.com.au/analytics/`.

We should see a fairly simple web page with information regarding Google's Analytics service. We already know what the service does, so most of this isn't important. Click on the button on the top-right corner of the page that says **create an account**. If you already have an account, simply **Sign in** at this point:

Sign in or create an account

After this, click on **create an account** and follow the on screen instructions to finish the account creation process.

Once signed in, you should see an empty tree structure. This is where our apps will be displayed and will allow us to view our app's data and stats. We need to create a new app listing so we can generate our app key.

To do this, go to the **Admin** tab at the top of the page:

Here, we can see a large amount of options regarding accounts, properties (apps), and the view. In the **Property** section, click on the drop-down list that says **All apps**. Then, select the option at the bottom that says **Create new property**:

This will take us to a new page where we can create a new app listing. Follow the on screen instructions to create the new app listing and fill in all the information. Make sure to select the **Mobile App** option and not the website option.

Once the information is filled in, click on the **Get Tracking ID** button.

We should then be taken to a new page where we can see the tracking ID of the app listing. Copy this key to your keyboard and open GameMaker now.

Once again, we need to export an extension from a demo. Go to the **Demos** tab in the GameMaker welcome screen. Then, open the **Analytics** branch and select the **Google Analytics** project.

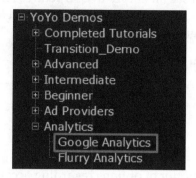

Click on **Create Project** to download and open the demo.

Once the project is open, open the **Extensions** branch on the resource tree and right-click on the **GoogleAnlyticsExt** extension. Then, select **Export Extension** from the drop-down list that appears:

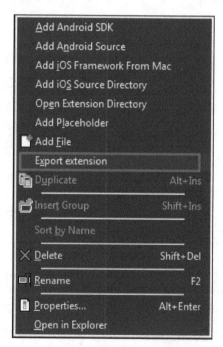

Save it somewhere on your computer and then open up your actual game project in GameMaker.

Right-click on the extensions listing in the resource tree and choose **Import Extension** from the drop-down list. Then, navigate to and load the analytics extension. This should add the Google Analytics extension that is ready for use.

Now, the only thing we need to do is initialize the extension. Open up your main control object and on a new line, add the `GoogleAnalytics_Init` function. For the first argument, paste the app ID from the Google Analytics website. The second argument is to ask if this is a dry run. A dry run is a run of the game that does not send any events even if told to do so. Set this to `0` to allow events to run.

That's all we actually need to do to have stats show on the Google Analytics website, as location data and general stats are all automatic from this point on.

However, if we wish to get a more in-depth view of what people are doing, we can send events. An event is any moment where the player might press a button or reach an achievement. It can be anything, really. To send an event, use the `GoogleAnalytics_SendEvent` function. In the arguments, you must give the event a category, an action (what happened?), and a label (extra information). The event will then show in the Google Analytics application stats when it's triggered.

# Exporting a game

One of the main parts of making a game of any form is exporting or compiling the final program into something usable by an audience. In GameMaker, we have multiple options for this, some more complicated than others. Some exports require external programs and software development kits to work (the Windows platform, however, is extremely simple).

The first step of exporting a game is, of course, making a game to export. This may be a prototype, an incomplete demo, or a full feature game ready for release. The only thing necessary to actually export to the Windows platform is at least one room.

To change the export platform that GameMaker will use, simply change the target shown at the top of the GameMaker interface:

Set this to **Windows** if it's not already done.

At this point, there are two options to export our game. We can click on the **File** drop-down menu at the top-left corner of the GameMaker interface and select **Create Application**:

Or, we can also use the export application button on the main toolbar .

Both of these options will open up Windows Explorer, allowing us to decide where to save the compiled game.

Before saving the game, though, it's important to know that we actually have three options for compiling at this point. At the bottom of the Explorer window, we have the **Save as type**: drop-down list. Clicking on this shows us three export options that we have available. You can see this in the following screenshot:

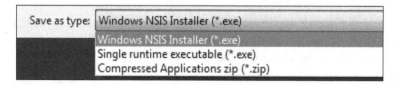

- **Windows NSIS Installer (*.exe)**: This option exports the game in the form of an installer. When running the installer, it will then export the final game and its needed files to the user's desired location, much like a normal software installer.

- **Single runtime executable (*.exe)**: This option exports the game as an all-in-one executable file. It runs completely on its own with all required files built directly into the executable file. This is not recommended for a final release project as it may be flagged as a virus by Windows and other antivirus software.

- **Compressed Applications zip (*.zip)**: This option exports the game in a compressed zip folder. The game will be packaged into a zip folder with all of its required files.

Select whichever of these options best suits the situation and then click on **Save** to export the game.

Every platform is different in its requirements; for example, the Android module requires the Android developers' kit. There is detailed documentation on setting up each module on the YoYo Games Knowledge Base website at `http://help.yoyogames.com/forums`.

# Publishing your game

Once a game has been created, exported, and ready for release, it's time to publish the game and share it with people. There are many ways to go about this and each platform has its own options. The Windows platform is the cheapest and easiest option, which makes it the most common with GameMaker developers.

Publishing a game is the process of releasing the game to the public and allowing people to play it through some means. This could be on a personal website or by using a distribution service. Any game made with GameMaker is free to distribute as you wish, so distribution options are ultimately limitless.

# YoYo Player

The YoYo Player is a new game distribution service from YoYo Games. This allows people who own GameMaker to upload their games for other people to play. The YoYo Player is often referred to as the GameMaker version of Steam.

Before we can upload a game, we must first have a player account. This can be created from directly inside the YoYo Player itself when we are prompted to log in. We can also make an account by going to `https://player.yoyogames.com`.

Simply click on the **Register here** button and follow the on screen instructions to set up an account.

Once we have a normal player account and can log in, we need to create the developer account. This new account will be linked directly to the one we just made and will allow us to upload games to the YoYo Player.

To create a developer account, follow the instructions on the YoYo Games wiki at `http://help.yoyogames.com/entries/102307146-Player-Setting-Up-A-Developer-Account`.

Once we have a developer account, we can now export our games for use with the YoYo Player.

To export the game to the YoYo Player, open GameMaker and select the **GameMaker: Player** option from the **Target** list:

Then, click on the **Compile** button.

A new window will show, where we must either create a new game or select an existing game to update. In this case, we want to create a new game:

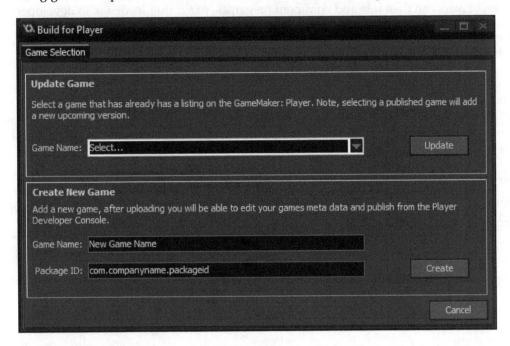

We must enter a name for the game and then edit the **Package ID** name to suit the template.

The ID name should be similar to com.companyname.packageid. This means if our company name was trap games, and our package name was jumper, then the package ID name would be com.trapgames.jumper.

Once the information is filled in, click on the **Create** button and go to the Player website at https://player.yoyogames.com.

Once on the site, click on your username at the top-right corner of the page and then click on your developer name from the drop-down list. This will take you to the developer console where you can edit the game's information, set a price, and finally publish the game for players to enjoy.

# Game Jolt

One of the best sites for game distribution is Game Jolt. Game Jolt is a site for indie developers to upload their creations both complete and in development for people to play. Players can then rate and comment on games, providing feedback to developers.

Game Jolt does not allow developers to sell games. All games must be free and a game listing must not link to another site for purchase. Game Jolt is a completely free site for both players and developers.

As Game Jolt is funded by ads, ads will display on game pages either before the game starts in a browser or on the side of the page. Developers get a percentage of ad revenue made through their games' pages and this revenue may be claimed through PayPal at any time.

Go to this URL to access the Game Jolt website at `http://gamejolt.com/`.

When uploading a game to Game Jolt, there are a number of upload types to choose from:

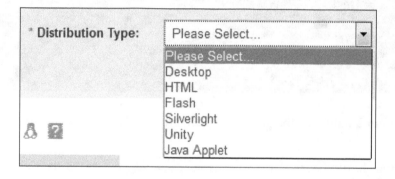

When uploading an executable file, select the **Desktop** option. This will be a direct download to the player's PC.

When uploading a HTML5 game, select the **HTML** option. This will run directly in the browser; all files must be packaged into a single compressed zip file when using this option.

The other options do not apply to games created in GameMaker.

Once a game is uploaded to Game Jolt, we are ready to make the page visible and in turn, make it open for people to download, play, and hopefully enjoy.

# Skill summary

Now that we have learned all the essential skills needed to use GameMaker: Studio, let's take a quick look back at the main skills we have learned:

- In *Chapter 1*, *Introducing GameMaker*, you learned about what GameMaker actually is and explored a little bit of history regarding previous versions. We then moved on to installing GameMaker on your computer, getting it ready for use.

- In *Chapter 2*, *Getting Started*, you learned about the license key for GameMaker and what it's used for, after which we proceeded to learn about the GameMaker interface. We looked at the Welcome window that first shows up when running GameMaker, the main toolbar, the drop-down menus, and finally, the resource tree.

- In *Chapter 3*, *Resource Management*, you learned about GameMaker's resources and ways to organize and manage them within our projects. These resources included sprites, sounds, backgrounds, paths, scripts, shaders, fonts, time lines, objects, rooms, extensions, and finally macros. We then looked into naming conventions that we could use to keep our resource names organized, and also how to create groups.

- In *Chapter 4*, *Objects*, we dived into the world of objects. We looked into how they are structured, how they work, and what can be done with them within our projects. We also used drag and drop functions to create a simple game.

- In *Chapter 5*, *The GameMaker Language*, you learned about GML. We started off learning about variables, their types, and how to make use of them. Then, you learned about functions, statements, and loops. Here, we saw how they are structured, how they are used, and what their most common uses are. Finally, you learned how to create a script and also why scripts are so useful when making a game in GameMaker.

- In *Chapter 6*, *Sprites*, we went into detail with sprites. You learned how to create them, how to animate them, what their properties are and do, and about common sizing techniques used. Then, you learned about how we can control sprites using the GameMaker Language code.

- In *Chapter 7*, *Making a Game*, we created our first actual game using GameMaker Language code and a combination of resources. We put all our past knowledge to work as we created resources and programmed objects to bring everything together into a simple game.

- In *Chapter 8, Debugging,* you learned about debugging games. We looked at the real errors produced by GameMaker and how to read them in order to find the problem. Then, you learned about drawing information to the screen in order to use visual aids to solve problems. We then looked into creating simple toggles to enable and disable features in our games. Finally, you learned about the GameMaker debugger and its use.

- Finally, we have *Chapter 9, Game Settings and Exporting,* which just so happens to be the chapter you are reading right now. In this chapter, you learned about the global game settings in every project, how to add advertising and analytics services to your games, how to export your games so they are ready to play, and finally, we looked at some of the publishing services we have available for use.

During the book, you learned many skills. The aforementioned are just the main skills and aims of each chapter; if you know how to do each of these, then each chapter was successful with its goal. Hopefully, you picked up some extra knowledge along the way.

# Taking this further

So, we have just finished learning about GameMaker essentials. How can we take this further and continue to learn and develop our skills?

The first and best way to learn more is to go over the book again and experiment with everything. Experimentation is the base of learning what can and cannot be done. For example, we could go back to *Chapter 7, Making a Game,* and change aspects of the game we created or even add more features to it.

The next step is research. While this book has covered the essential skills that should be enacted when using GameMaker, there is still much more that can be done. If you don't know how to do something, just search online and someone may very well have asked and solved the problem before. Learn from other people's mistakes and other people's questions.

Look to the official GameMaker Community for thousands of questions and answers on both simple and advanced topics. Feel free to write your own questions and post about your games in the correct subforums also. It's a good idea to become an active part of the community as this allows you to collect contacts, which can help you as you learn.

The GameMaker Community website is available at: http://gmc.yoyogames.com/

The final tip is patience. When making games, you will constantly run into problems and roadblocks, especially as a beginner. It's important to have patience; most problems can be overcome with a bit of research and persistence.

# Games made in GameMaker

If you have any concerns with what GameMaker can actually do and if it's a powerful enough engine for your game, take a look at some of the games on the GameMaker Showcase at `https://www.yoyogames.com/showcase`.

# GameMaker learning sites

While this book has taught us the essential skills of GameMaker, there is still so much more to learn. There are many websites available online where we can ask questions and learn more about GameMaker, and also how to achieve specific tasks inside of GameMaker.

# The GameMaker Community

The GameMaker community is one of the best places to ask questions and learn about GameMaker. Here, people ask questions on how to create deferent things, what things do, and how they can be used. More experienced user can then answer these questions.

# YouTube

YouTube is one of the best mediums through which to learn anything. There are hundreds of tutorials, showing how to create many different things in GameMaker such as turrets, role playing games, and so on. Here are some YouTube channels that have great tutorials for GameMaker:

- **Shaun Spalding**: `https://www.youtube.com/user/999Greyfox`
- **NT Games**: `https://www.youtube.com/user/xxNTGamesxx`
- **RealTutsGML**: `https://www.youtube.com/user/RealTutsGML/videos`

There are many more channels based around or including GameMaker tutorials. Above is just a selection of these channels.

# Summary

In this chapter, we learned how to set up advertisements in our applications, how to enable Google Analytics so we can see live stats on our applications, and also how to publish our games for other people to play offline and online.

This chapter concludes the end of this book on GameMaker essentials. You learned many things throughout this book and are now ready to enter the world of game development using GameMaker: Studio.

# Index

## N

**NT Games**
  URL 131

## O

**objects**
  creating 89, 90
**one-dimensional array 51**

## P

**parents**
  about 35
  and collisions 36
  making 35
**power of two technique 71**

## R

**RealTutsGML**
  URL 131
**repeat loop 56**
**resource management 15, 16**
**resource naming conventions**
  about 25
  three-letter code words 26
**resources**
  about 16
  backgrounds 19
  exporting 29, 30
  extensions 24
  fonts 22
  GameMaker resources, importing 29
  graphics, importing 28
  importing 28
  macros 24, 25
  objects 23
  organizing 27
  paths 20, 21
  rooms 24
  scripts 21
  scripts, exporting 30
  shaders 22
  sounds 18, 19
  sounds, importing 28

sprites 17
  timelines 22
**resources, organizing techniques**
  about 27
  groups 27
  sprite animations 27, 28
**resource tree**
  accessing 12, 13
**room**
  setting up 87, 88
  views 89
**room speed 34**

## S

**scripts**
  about 58
  argument hints 61
  arguments 60, 61
  creating 58
  executing 60
  naming 59
  value, returning 62, 63
  writing 59
**Shaun Spalding**
  URL 131
**show_debug_message function 108**
**skills**
  developing 130
**sound resource 18, 19**
**sprite_height variable 81**
**sprite_index variable 80**
**sprite options**
  about 66
  collision masks 67
  collision masks, editing 67-69
  sprite origins 66
  texture settings 70, 71
**sprites**
  about 72
  creating 85-87
  creating, from scratch 72-76
  effects, applying 77-80
**sprites, GameMaker Language**
  about 80
  alpha, setting 82

animation speed, setting 81
frame, setting 81
loading 65, 66
object's sprite, setting 80
offset, obtaining from 81
rotation, setting 82
scale, changing 82
subimages, finding 83
width and height 81
**sprite sizing techniques**
about 71
power of two 71
templates 72
**sprite_width variable 81**
**sprite_xoffset variable 81**
**sprite_yoffset variable 81**
**statements**
about 53
else if statement 55
else statement 54
if statement 53
**step event 34**

# T

**toggles**
applying 109
**two-dimensional array 51**

# V

**variables**
arrays 51
global variable 48
instance variable 47
local variable 48
macro 49

# W

**welcome window 7, 8**
**while loop 56**

# Y

**YouTube**
about 131
references, for tutorials 131
**YoYo Games**
URL 125
**YoYo Player**
about 125
developer account, creating 126
game, exporting to 126, 127
URL, for games 127

## Thank you for buying
# GameMaker Essentials

# About Packt Publishing

Packt, pronounced 'packed', published its first book, *Mastering phpMyAdmin for Effective MySQL Management*, in April 2004, and subsequently continued to specialize in publishing highly focused books on specific technologies and solutions.

Our books and publications share the experiences of your fellow IT professionals in adapting and customizing today's systems, applications, and frameworks. Our solution-based books give you the knowledge and power to customize the software and technologies you're using to get the job done. Packt books are more specific and less general than the IT books you have seen in the past. Our unique business model allows us to bring you more focused information, giving you more of what you need to know, and less of what you don't.

Packt is a modern yet unique publishing company that focuses on producing quality, cutting-edge books for communities of developers, administrators, and newbies alike. For more information, please visit our website at www.packtpub.com.

# About Packt Open Source

In 2010, Packt launched two new brands, Packt Open Source and Packt Enterprise, in order to continue its focus on specialization. This book is part of the Packt Open Source brand, home to books published on software built around open source licenses, and offering information to anybody from advanced developers to budding web designers. The Open Source brand also runs Packt's Open Source Royalty Scheme, by which Packt gives a royalty to each open source project about whose software a book is sold.

# Writing for Packt

We welcome all inquiries from people who are interested in authoring. Book proposals should be sent to author@packtpub.com. If your book idea is still at an early stage and you would like to discuss it first before writing a formal book proposal, then please contact us; one of our commissioning editors will get in touch with you.

We're not just looking for published authors; if you have strong technical skills but no writing experience, our experienced editors can help you develop a writing career, or simply get some additional reward for your expertise.

## GameMaker Game Programming with GML

ISBN: 978-1-78355-944-2          Paperback: 350 pages

Learn GameMaker Language programming concepts and script integration with GameMaker: Studio through hands-on, playable examples

1. Write and utilize scripts to help organize and speed up your game production workflow.

2. Display important user interface components such as score, health, and lives.

3. Play sound effects and music, and create particle effects to add some spice to your projects.

4. Build your own example match-three puzzle and platform games.

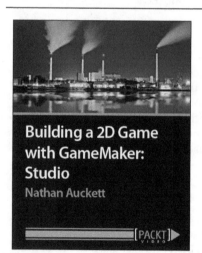

## Building a 2D Game with GameMaker: Studio [Video]

ISBN: 978-1-78355-876-6          Duration: 02:13 hours

All you need to know to get started with GameMaker: Studio

1. Learn how to use GameMaker: Studio and its interface.

2. Program in Game Maker Language (GML).

3. Create your very own artificial intelligence.

## Unity 2D Game Development Cookbook

ISBN: 978-1-78355-359-4      Paperback: 256 pages

Over 50 hands-on recipes that leverage the features of Unity to help you create 2D games and game prototypes

1.  Create 2D games right from importing assets to setting them up in Unity and adding them to your game scenes.

2.  Program the game logic and events as well as the game controls and user interface using the C# scripting language and Monodevelop.

3.  A step-by-step guide written in a practical format to take advantage of the many features available in Unity.

## Learning Cocos2d-JS Game Development

ISBN: 978-1-78439-007-5      Paperback: 188 pages

Learn to create robust and engaging cross-platform HTML5 games using Cocos2d-JS

1.  Create HTML5 games running both on desktop and mobile devices, played with both mouse and touch controls.

2.  Add advanced features such as realistic physics, particle effects, scrolling, tweaking, sound effects, background music, and more to your games.

3.  Build exciting cross-platform games and build a memory game, an endless runner and a physics-driven game.

Please check **www.PacktPub.com** for information on our titles

CPSIA information can be obtained
at www.ICGtesting.com
Printed in the USA
FSHW02n0556280718
50870FS

9 781784 396121